SSSP

Springer
Series in
Social
Psychology

SSSP

Daniel Bar-Tal

Group Beliefs

*A Conception for Analyzing Group
Structure, Processes, and Behavior*

Springer-Verlag New York Berlin Heidelberg
London Paris Tokyo Hong Kong

Daniel Bar-Tal
School of Education
Tel-Aviv University
Tel-Aviv 69978
Israel

Library of Congress Cataloging-in-Publication Data
Bar-Tal, Daniel.
    Group beliefs: a conception for analyzing group structure,
processes, and behavior/Daniel Bar-Tal.
        p.   cm. – (Springer series in social psychology)
    ISBN 0-387-97085-1 (U.S.)
    1. Social groups.   2. Belief and doubt.   3. Attitude (Psychology)
4. Social values.   I. Title.   II. Series.
HM131.B28   1989
302.3 – dc20   89-11527

Typeset by Caliber Design Planning, Inc.
Printed and bound by R.R. Donnelley & Sons, Harrisonburg, Virginia.
Printed in the United States of America.

9 8 7 6 5 4 3 2 1

ISBN 0-387-97085-1 Springer-Verlag New York Berlin Heidelberg
ISBN 3-540-97085-1 Springer-Verlag Berlin Heidelberg New York

To Zosia, Yakub, Hagar, Yoram, Daphne,
Shai, and Tamar (Bar-Tals)
who have a group belief of helping and supporting.

Preface

The work on group beliefs stems from my interest in the formation of social knowledge by individuals and groups. On the basis of the specialization in the early phases of my career, which concerned the knowledge children utilize to explain their helping behavior or their academic successes and failures, the present focus on the processes of knowledge acquisition and its change has emerged. Within this framework, I have had the opportunity to combine my interests in history, politics, and social psychology by paying special attention to political beliefs shared by group members. The idea of writing about group beliefs crystallized several years ago.

It all began one day in January 1985. Yaacov Trope from the Hebrew University of Jerusalem called and asked me to give a colloquium about my work in political psychology. At that time, after abandoning my interest in prosocial behavior and achievement attributions, I focused on examining separately various specific political beliefs such as patriotism, siege mentality, and conflict. The invitation to give a colloquium caused me to try to integrate these separate ideas into one coherent framework. It was then that I began to use the term group beliefs.

However, the meaning of the concept which I first proposed is different from the one presented in this book. From the present perspective, my first proposal was not successful. Although I was confident that the beliefs I studied had something in common, the nature of the commonality was not yet clear to me.

The next opportunity to come up with a better conception of group beliefs came with the help of Jeff Rubin, who agreed to include my presentation about group beliefs in the International Society of Political Psychology (ISPP) program for the 1986 meeting in Amsterdam. After working on the manuscript for several months under hectic Israeli conditions, I sent the draft of the paper to Icek Ajzen, Yehuda Amir, Nehemia Friedland, Paul Haré, and Shalom Schwartz for review. The critical reactions came quickly, and 3 months before the meeting the presentation was still disjointed.

At this point it is necessary to note that my brother, Yoram, a close friend and a colleague, was the most helpful supporter of my ideas about group beliefs. He patiently listened and provided constructive, encouraging feedback which energized me to continue to think, in spite of the initial failures. And so one day, as introductory psychology textbooks describe, on an evening walk with Yoram, an "aha effect" occurred. Ideas crossed my mind and the basic conception presented in this book was formed. The paper was quickly written and presented at the ISPP meeting. David Sears, Jaap Rabbie, and Leonard Saxe were strict discussants, providing important comments that helped me to improve the original conception.

Then I began a period of collecting material, expanding ideas, and forming new ones. It was only during my sabbatical at Brandeis University that I had the opportunity and conditions to write the chapters of the book. Without the hospitable environment of the Psychology Department at Brandeis, I would not have been able to finish the book so quickly. The Brandeis Psychology Department provided me with ideal writing conditions and with all the necessary help. In this vein, Judy Woodman from Brandeis deserves special thanks for typing and retyping the whole manuscript within a framework of time that allowed me to finish it.

The School of Education at Tel-Aviv University not only was patient with this type of work, but also provided financial aid for assistants and for typing the final revision, which was done by Alice Zilcha. Thanks to her.

Bill Stone read the whole manuscript, and his comments were of great help in the final revision. Also a number of colleagues read various chapters of the book and provided valuable feedback which helped to improve the final product. My gratitude is expressed to Icek Ajzen, Yehuda Bauer, Michael Berbaum, Susan Fiske, Ken Gergen, Carl Graumann, Gerda Lederer, John Levine, Miriam Lewin, Leslie Zebrowitz-McArthur, Serge Moscovici, Jerry Samet, Ervin Staub, and Lloyd Strickland. This is the place to mention that Ken Gergen encouraged me to write a postscript in the book.

The help of Ronit Wienman and Shelley Bloomfield-Shoham from Tel-Aviv University in the bibliographical search is gladly acknowledged. Michael A. Cohen and David Adler from Brandeis University helped to edit and type portions of the manuscript. Of special value was the help of Dikla Antebi, who assisted in the collection of bibliographical information.

Finally, the staff of Springer-Verlag deserves special thanks for encouraging me to write the book, patiently waiting for the final product, and helping to turn it into a readable volume.

Tel-Aviv, Israel   Daniel Bar-Tal

Contents

Introduction

Two of the important concepts frequently used by social psychologists are the terms *belief* and *group*. Though much effort has been directed toward studying them, they have been rarely examined as related phenomena. While beliefs have been studied mainly on an intraindividual level, the traditional analysis of groups has paid relatively little attention to beliefs as a group phenomenon. Within the first framework, social psychologists have been preoccupied with studying beliefs as characteristics of an individual. The studies of dissonance, impression formation, attribution, social cognition, or attitudes have mainly focused on the microprocesses of structure, formation, and change within a single person (see, for example, Abelson, Aronson, McGuire, Newcomb, Rosenberg, & Tannenbaum, 1968; Fiske & Taylor, 1984; Krech & Crutchfield, 1948; Markus & Zajonc, 1985; Wyer & Srull, 1984). At the same time, the students of groups, after the fiasco of McDougall's (1920) attempt to introduce the concept of *group mind*, have not tried seriously to study cognitive products as group characteristics (Allport, 1968).

Although beliefs do not exist apart from individuals, they cannot be studied only on an individual's level. *Individuals who live in groups hold common beliefs which define their reality, not only as persons, but also as group members. This reality becomes especially important when group members become aware that they share it. There may be an important difference for the group between the situations when a belief is held by one member of the group, or even by all the members, who are not aware of sharing this belief, and the situations when a belief is held by all the members or a portion of them, who are aware of this sharing.*

Beliefs in the former situations may be influential for the group as a whole, as in the cases when a leader's beliefs affect the followers. However, this does not provide sufficient explanation for the binding element that allows group members to perceive themselves as a group, to develop collective identity, to have common tradition, and to act in a coordinated manner. As Lewin (1947) pointed out, "It seems to be impossible to predict group behavior without taking into account group goals, group standards, group values, and the way a group 'sees' its own situation and that of other groups" (p. 12).

Lewin's idea is based on the view that individuals not only think, feel, and see things from a personal perspective, but also from the standpoint of the group of which they are a part. As noted by Sherif (1966), group members share attitudes, sentiments, aspirations, goals, values, and norms which pertain to group's life. This view is repeatedly emphasized by social scientists. For example, Mead (1934) suggested that people perceive, judge, or think according to the frame of reference of the group in which they are participating. Accordingly, the socialized person is also, to some extent, a microcosm of society. That is, group members share norms, values, and goals which allow them to define the world from the perspectives they share with others.

Beliefs that are known to be shared by group members may have important cognitive, affective, and behavioral implications both for group members as individuals and for the group as a whole. Specifically, these beliefs may contribute to the explanation of the behavioral direction that the group takes; the influence that group members exert on their leaders, and vice versa; the coordination of group activities; the structure of the group; and the intensity and involvement of group members with certain attitudes. First of all, however, shared beliefs have the distinctive potential for determining the boundaries of the group. Thus, it is suggested that in the same way that understanding an individual (his/her attitudes and behavior) requires knowledge of his/her personal beliefs, understanding a group's structure, attitudes, and behaviors requires a cognizance of the group's beliefs.

It was Asch (1952) who pointed out that:

> Group facts must have their foundation in individuals; group consciousness, group purpose, and group values have an existence in individuals, and in them alone. But they cease to be "merely" individual facts by virtue of their reference to others. It follows that a group process is neither the sum of individual activity nor a fact added to the activities of individuals. (p. 252)

In line with the above view, it is suggested that the study of shared beliefs by group members should come as an addition to the traditional interest in a group which concerns mainly such topics as structural qualities of a group, environmental features of group activities, group influence, individual characteristics of group members, group performance, and group interaction patterns (e.g., Blumberg, Hare, Kent, & Davies, 1983; Cartwright & Zander, 1968; Golembiewski, 1962; Hare, 1976; McGrath & Altman, 1966; Shaw, 1976; Stogdill, 1959; Verba, 1961). Thus, the present approach neither replaces the previously mentioned topics of interest nor precludes other disciplinary analyses; it points out the importance of group beliefs in studying groups.

The present book attempts to call attention to cognitive products of beliefs as group characteristics. Specifically, it introduces a new concept of group beliefs that accounts for the fact that group members share beliefs and consider some of them as defining their "groupness." Moreover, it suggests that the proposed conception of group beliefs sheds a new light on the structure and processes of groups. That is, the conceptual framework presented here can be used not only as a description of group characteristics, but also in the analysis of changes that a group may go through.

The book begins with the discussion of beliefs, including their epistemological foundation, definition, and characteristics (chapter 1). Chapter 2 reviews various past attempts to deal with the cognitive group products. It focuses on conceptions proposed at the end of the previous century and the beginning of the present one. Using this basis, the conception of group beliefs is presented in chapter 3. This chapter not only defines the concept and indicates ways to study it, but also discusses its implication for a group perspective. Subsequently, the contents of group beliefs are illustrated and characteristics of group beliefs are described (chapter 4).

Chapters 5 and 6 analyze the relations between various group processes and group beliefs. Chapter 5 suggests that the formation and maintenance of groups is based, among other factors, on group beliefs. That is, a necessary condition for group formation and existence is the formulation and preservation of group beliefs. Chapter 6 analyzes group changes such as group mergence, subgrouping, split (schism), and disintegration as being underlain by the dynamics of group beliefs.

Chapter 7 provides an example of group beliefs. The selected case illustrates group beliefs of a nation. The case discusses the delegitimizing beliefs of Germans about Jews during the Nazi era (1933–1945). It tries to demonstrate that group beliefs are a useful conceptual tool that can also explain large groups' behaviors.

The last chapter (chapter 8) discusses the implications of the presented conception for the study of groups. In this discussion, a special attempt is made to point out the contribution of the presented concept for social psychology in general. Finally, the Postscript suggests that the present framework may be useful in analyzing the group dynamics of scientists, as they produce scientific knowledge. In some respects, this part brings the volume full circle, since the first chapter outlines the philosophical basis of the present conception.

The book is written by a social psychologist for social scientists. Although my foundations in social psychology are identifiable, an attempt was made to write a book with implications beyond one discipline. Groups exist in various settings, in different systems, and are a subject of interest for psychologists, sociologists, anthropologists, political scientists, and other specialists. The concept of group beliefs characterizes all collectives whose members agree that they constitute a group. It can be applied to the analysis of small groups, organizations, and even to large groups such as religious denominations or nations.

Individuals are at the same time members of various groups—small and large groups. Each group has group beliefs, which its members acquire. Individuals, thus, store different group beliefs, some of which may be of great importance for them, irrespective of group size.

The selected case presented in chapter 7 focuses on specific group beliefs of a large group—a nation. This was a difficult choice, since the analysis of a nation's group beliefs is especially problematic, as will be pointed out in the book. Although there is an enormous quantity of other examples of group beliefs pertaining to various groups such as sects, interest groups, or political parties, many of which are described in the book, I decided to devote a chapter to a case of a nation's group beliefs. This "mission impossible" stems from my deep interest in beliefs that are part of a nation's members' cognitive repertoire, determine their reality, shape their attitudes, and above all influence their behavior as a group, especially of the leadership (see for example Bar-Tal, D., 1986, 1988, 1989a, 1989b, in press-a; Bar-Tal, D., & Antebi, 1989; Bar-Tal, D., & Geva, 1985; Bar-Tal, D., Kruglanski, & Klar, 1989; Klar, Bar-Tal, D., & Kruglanski, 1988). In spite of the difficulty of studying group beliefs of nations, I do believe that they exist, and anyone who desires to understand policies, leaders' decisions, or nations' actions also has to take them into account.

Thus, the objective of this book is to open a new avenue of understanding of group behavior for the students of groups, in general. Therefore, a special effort was made not only to rely on writings of social scientists from different disciplines, but also to provide examples from different types of groups. This was done because the study of group behavior is an important endeavor. Humans spend a considerable portion of their lives in groups, and group identity is an inseparable part of an individual's self-perception as a group member. The psychological meaning of group identity is that group members share beliefs that are considered as unique characteristics of the group.

Chapter 1

Nature of Beliefs

This book is concerned with the contents of the beliefs (i.e., knowledge) that are shared by group members. Since group beliefs is the book's major theme, it is important first to describe a conception of knowledge that serves as a basis for further analysis of beliefs (units of knowledge, either on the individual's or group's level). This description serves as an "identification card" that outlines the fundamental premises that underlie the present conceptual framework.

Epistemological Basis of Beliefs

The study of individuals' beliefs is a study of human knowledge, since according to the present approach, beliefs are units of knowledge. The totality of these beliefs constitutes the system of knowledge. The term *knowledge*, as used in the present book, includes such diversely used cognitive terms as "hypotheses," "decisions," "inferences," "values," "intentions," "ideologies," "norms," or "impressions." All of these terms denote specific categories of knowledge.

Some psychologists use the term *cognition* interchangeably with the term *knowledge* (e.g., Shaw & Bransford, 1977; Solso, 1973). For them, knowledge implies all of the stored cognitions. However, while cognition also usually indicates to psychologists a structure or the process of knowing, *knowledge denotes a set of beliefs to which individuals attribute at least some truth.* The latter term thus refers to the subjective internal state of knowing. *Knowledge encompasses all the beliefs accumulated through our own experience, thinking, or as a result of contact with other individuals or their products.* It includes scientific knowledge as well as common sense knowledge in everyday life (Berger & Luckmann, 1966). This broad definition deviates from the traditional definition of knowledge proposed by philosophers who differentiate between knowledge and beliefs (e.g., Griffiths, 1967; Hintikka, 1962). They view knowledge as consisting of justified true beliefs, while an ordinary belief (i.e., not justified) is only a subjective state of mind concerned with a proposition.

The study of knowledge has received special attention throughout the history of science. First philosophers and, more recently, behavioral scientists have attempted to understand the essence of knowledge. Philosophy has designated an area of interest called epistemology for those who have been preoccupied with theories of knowledge. Philosophers from Plato and Aristotle, through Descartes, Locke, and Kant, to Russell and Popper have tried to assess the nature of knowledge and determine its sources and validity. In contrast, behavioral scientists, including cognitive psychologists, have focused not so much on the philosophical questions of essence and validity of knowledge, but more on its structure in the mind, specific contents, acquisition process, and effects on various individuals' reactions.

Through the years, thousands of pages have been written about human knowledge. It is beyond the scope of this chapter to review the various views, theories, and approaches to this important subject. Nevertheless, the ideas presented in this book have a founding base: They are influenced by the nonjustificational position propagated by the new philosophy of science (Weimer, 1979). This approach will be summarized.

Nonjustificational Approach to Science

The nonjustificational approach to science maintains that all human beliefs, including scientific theories, are conjectural. Beliefs can neither be proven true nor ultimately justified by an appeal to any ultimate authority (Feyerabend, 1981; Kuhn, 1970; Lakatos & Musgrave, 1970; Popper, 1959, 1963). This view suggests that "knowledge claims, whether scientific or otherwise, are always *fallible*; anything in both common sense and the 'body of science' is subject to criticism and consequent revision or rejection, *at all times and for all time*" (Weimer, 1979, pp. 39–40). Since we lack any objective criteria to prove knowledge (i.e., sets of beliefs) with appropriate epistemological authority, we must reject the notion either that knowledge has to be proven in order to be genuine or that the use of proof necessarily implies truth.

The basic assumption underlying the nonjustificational rejection of truth by proof lies in the conviction that proofs as provided in science are presupposed by theories that are held by individuals. Popper (1959) originated this argument by suggesting that "we can utter no scientific statement that does not go far beyond what can be known with certainty 'on the basis of immediate experience'. . . . Every description uses universal names (or symbols, or ideas); every statement has the character of a theory, of a hypothesis" (pp. 94–95). Along this line, Lakatos (1970) argued that predictions are generated by sets of theories and hypotheses that tell the scientists what is to count as an observation of a relevant datum. Thus, observations are not objective, but profoundly shaped by scientists' views, theories, and conceptions. With this basis in mind, it has also been suggested that scientists focus on only a few of the limitless features of the environment when they investigate a phenomenon, since their observations are always based on their own limited knowledge (Popper,

1963). Evaluation of truth in knowledge claims requires the understanding of how it is justified, not the degree of its accurate representation of reality.

Accordingly, the rationality of science cannot be expressed by any method of absolute proof or falsification, but rather by criticizing or testing the consistency between any relevant empirical and theoretical information and the position that one entertains at the time. This is "merely a very important aspect of the more general idea of intersubjective criticism, or, in other words, of the idea of mutual rational control by critical discussion" (Popper, 1959, p. 44). It implies that the aim of a scientist is not to prove a given proposition, "but rather the marshaling of 'good reasons' in its behalf. And the 'good reasons' are never justifications of the claim, only conjectures that are relevant to its assessment" (Weimer, 1979, p. 41).

This view of knowledge has not only been propagated by philosophers, but also accepted, with notable differences, by several social psychologists. For example, Gergen (1982), Kruglanski (1989), and Manicas and Secord (1983) have adhered to the main principles of the analysis of knowledge presented here. Gergen views knowledge as constructed by individuals. He states that "knowledge would appear vitally dependent on the vicissitudes of social negotiation. Its constraints would not essentially be experiential but social" (p. 201). Kruglanski characterized knowledge with the metaphor of Lego blocks. According to him, "the Lego metaphor connotes the considerable diversity in types of things that we may know. Our general repertory of knowledge is likened to a set of temporarily stable configurations" (p. 10). Furthermore, he assumed that "knowledge is actively constructed by ourselves in the course of our interaction with others, and that the constraints set in its various forms are *subjective* (having to do with things we regard as facts) rather than objective. This means that in principle nearly 'anything goes', and hardly any conceptual configuration is prohibited *a priori*" (p. 10). Similarly, Manicas and Secord argue that "knowledge is a social and historical product. . . . This means that there is no preinterpreted 'given' and that the test of truth cannot be 'correspondence'" (p. 401). Individuals construct their beliefs in social context, and groups determine their own criteria to decide what beliefs are accepted as truth for them.

The described nonjustificational approach implies that (a) the scope of possible beliefs cannot be limited, (b) beliefs considered to be true can later be viewed as false and vice versa, (c) individuals may hold different beliefs and may attribute different levels of truth to the same beliefs, and (d) beliefs are organized. These implications will be discussed further.

Unlimited scope of beliefs. The scope of beliefs is infinite. It has no a priori boundaries and no fantasy can establish its limits. Human thoughts are endless in their scope. All the time, new ideas, opinions, or conceptions (i.e., beliefs) are formed. Beliefs that were not even in the human repertoire a short time ago are considered as examined facts today, and there is no way to know what will be the content of beliefs tomorrow.

Within the presented framework, any belief can be considered knowledge. Both individuals and groups have their own sets of beliefs that they consider to be knowledge. This view makes the problem even more complicated, since it is impossible to encompass all the beliefs of today. The combined beliefs of the more than 4 billion individuals who are alive today, and the accumulated knowledge from the past that has survived and is available today, are of such scope that they already today can be considered as infinite. The imagination probably cannot even grasp what the scope of future knowledge will be.

The accumulated knowledge can be categorized in any number of ways. For example, philosophers make a distinction between knowledge by acquaintance and knowledge by description (Russell, 1948), or between knowing *how* and knowing *that* (Ryle, 1949). Beliefs can be aggregated in numerous ways to various categories and each category can be further subdivided into even more categories. Human beings as individuals and groups devise their own ways of categorization. The numerous categorizations are derived from different contents of knowledge that people possess and different ways that people view the same knowledge.

Changing status of beliefs. What human beings consider as their knowledge changes from time to time and differs from group to group (Kaufman, 1960; Sayers, 1985). Beliefs that were once considered ignorant or faulty are viewed as facts and verity today and vice versa. Also, what is considered as superstition and myth by one group is viewed as truth and holy writ by another. This feature implies the dynamic nature of beliefs. On the one hand, beliefs are continuously added, omitted, and/or modified, while, on the other hand, the extent of attributed truth to any given belief may also change.

This case for relativism begins with anthropological and historical observations. From these two disciplines we have learned that beliefs about the world differ from culture to culture and from one historical epoch to another. The objectivity of beliefs is determined within a particular social framework of thought. It is a judgment that is unavoidably relative to a particular social framework, though knowledge is not based on mere product of discourse, without any basis in the environmental reality. The environment around us is real, but human beings have physical, anatomical, and psychological limitations in their cognizance of the environment. It is assumed that individuals perceive the world only through their own interpretation and understanding, which are stamped by the place and time they live in. Thus, perception of reality cannot be separated from its social context. Any theory of beliefs must take into account the social context in which beliefs are formed. Objectivity and truth are declared by the given society and held as such. But often they are limited to a certain time, place, or situation (e.g., Berger & Luckmann, 1966; Mannheim, 1954; Merton, 1957).

The idea that knowledge is relative is not alien to social psychologists. Gergen (1973) went as far as suggesting that social psychology is an historical science. According to him, social knowledge changes with time and does not generally transcend its historical boundaries. Similarly, Triandis (1972, 1976) emphasized cultural differences with regard to contents of knowledge in his writings. Human knowledge, according to Triandis, is culturally determined. Individuals in different cultures have different experiences, form different knowledge, and later approach information in the environment differently.

Individual differences. Individuals form their beliefs on the basis of their own experiences and attach meanings to them accordingly. Since each person has his/her own unique set of experiences, individuals differ in the set of beliefs that they acquire and form. Each individual perceives, experiences, and understands the world in his/her own way (McGinn, 1983; Poole, 1972). This view implies that individuals are captives of their own perspectives. Individuals often perceive and evaluate the same events, objects, or people differently. Their knowledge is objective for themselves and provides their reality. What is considered as real and true is real and true for themselves.

The accumulated evidence in psychology supports the described view of beliefs. Psychologists, especially cognitive psychologists, have long realized that each person forms a unique set of knowledge on the basis of his/her own experiences, cognitive capacity, and motivations (e.g., Bartlett, 1932; Bruner, Goodnow, & Austin, 1956; Krech & Crutchfield, 1948). As Neisser (1967) noted, ". . . The world of experience is produced by the man who experiences it. . . . Whatever we know about reality has been *mediated*, not only by the organs of sense but by complex systems which interpret and reinterpret sensory information" (p. 3).

The process of knowledge formation takes place from the moment the infant comes to the earth's light until the moment of death. In this process, individuals continually acquire, revise, add, omit, and change their beliefs on the basis of their abilities and motivations (Bar-Tal & Saxe, in press). However, this process is always based on previously acquired beliefs, into which are elaborated newly formed beliefs (Bransford, 1980). The outcomes of perception, interpretation, and evaluation depend on previously acquired beliefs. Thus, the contents of new beliefs always depend on the contents of beliefs formed in the past. This process assures that no two people will have *exactly* the same repertoire of beliefs (see Markus & Zajonc, 1985; Fiske & Taylor, 1984).

The description is even more complex when one takes into account that out of the available stored beliefs, only a few are accessible at any given time. To a large extent, these beliefs determine the contents of judgments, identifications, or impressions that an individual makes (Higgins & King, 1981). It is difficult to determine a priori what beliefs will be accessible at any given time, since the accessibility of beliefs is not only influenced by external information, but also by internal factors such as the flow of associations and motivations.

Although knowledge is subjective, it should be recognized that individuals who have similar experiences or collect the same information may develop partially common knowledge. Individuals share beliefs mostly as members of the same group. Within this framework, they live the same experiences and are provided with the same information. The extent of knowledge commonality depends on the extent of group members' participation in the group's life. The more intensive and extensive the participation of the group members, the more beliefs they share. On another level, however, the development of mass communication has facilitated the sharing of knowledge, not only among members of the same group, but also among individuals living in different parts of the world who are members of different groups.

Beliefs are organized. Human knowledge does not consist of an amalgam of unrelated beliefs, but rather of systematically organized sets of interrelated beliefs. That is, individuals group beliefs into categories to provide structure and meaning. These categories consist of interrelated beliefs that allow for a coherent view of the world. The organization of beliefs is fluid and dynamic. The categories expand or contract and new categories are added continuously. The categories are constructed around certain themes that have meaning for the individual.

The proposition that individuals organize their knowledge was greatly advanced by Gestalt psychologists. In their view, perceived phenomena are organized wholes. They convincingly argued that for perceptual organization, the way the parts are seen is determined by the configuration of the whole. Modern cognitive psychology has advanced these ideas. Knowledge, or cognition as it is often labeled, is viewed as being structured and organized into representational categories called schemata, symbols, frames, maps, or images, to name just a few. They represent the world of the individuals (e.g., Bransford, 1980; Neisser, 1967). Individuals acquire new information and form new ideas which are classified and stored according to the assigned category. Later, such an organization enables a retrieval of knowledge and its use in various inferences.

Content-Process Distinction

Of special importance for the present analysis is the distinction between contents of knowledge and process of knowledge formation. *Contents of knowledge refer to beliefs that a person uses to characterize people, behaviors, events, objects, places, or situations.* Contents are people's representations of reality. *Processes of knowledge formation refer to the sequence of operations performed by individuals as they form a given bit of knowledge.* The description may focus on overt or covert behaviors in the process of knowledge formation. Processes of knowledge formation consist of the acquisition of knowledge and change of knowledge, which in social psychological terms consist of such specific processes as impression formation, attitude change, social perception, and social influence.

Both contents and processes may be formulated on different levels of generality. Contents of knowledge can either refer to specific objects, such as a tree, a stone, a particular event, or a specific person, or refer to general categories, such as reinforcement, law, or symbol. The generality of the content does not necessarily imply its universality. Specific contents, as well as categories, can be held by a particular person or shared by a number of individuals, by a whole group, or even by the majority of human beings. A process of knowledge acquisition can also be either specific, such as a description of how someone received particular news, or general, when it is described in general terms, such as a sequence of operations in the decision-making process or impression formation, without referring to specific decisions or impressions. Psychologists have made great efforts to describe general processes of knowledge formation.

The distinction between contents and processes of knowledge is not a new one. A number of social psychologists have paid attention to this important distinction (e.g., Kruglanski, 1980; McClelland, 1955; Newell & Simon, 1972; Scott, Osgood,

& Peterson, 1979). For example, Kruglanski proposed a description of the universal process of knowledge acquisition, which takes place irrespective of the contents that are processed. According to him, the epistemic process of knowledge acquisition consists of two phases. First, there is the *cognitive generation phase*, which addresses the issue of generation of the contents of knowledge. Second, there is the *cognitive validation phase* in which a degree of confidence is attributed to the generated contents. The first phase of cognitive generation focuses on what was metaphorically described by Karl Popper (1972) using a "search light" analogy of human consciousness, that is, the contents of knowledge that come to mind at a certain time. Since the human mental capacity is limited at any given time, individuals can only generate a restricted number of contents on the basis of incoming information and/or their own insights.

The second phase of cognitive validation is performed via the consistency principle. An individual tests the generated cognitions or their implications against the evidence (i.e., stored beliefs) he/she possesses. If the evidence is logically consistent with the implications, then the individual's confidence in the validity of this cognition is strengthened. But if the evidence is inconsistent, then the individual's confidence in the cognition may be undermined. A central postulate of this theory is that the process does not have a natural point of termination. In principle, at least, it is always possible to come up with a number of alternative hypotheses (contents) which may be consistent with the same body of evidence. In reality, however, individuals end the epistemic process with regard to certain cognitions by bestowing on them a certain degree of confidence without considering further alternatives. This cognitive phenomenon is termed *epistemic freezing*. In contrast, the phenomenon of entertaining alternative contents, validating them, and eventually replacing previous beliefs with the new contents represents *epistemic unfreezing*.

The presented view differentiates between studies of knowledge acquisition processes and knowledge contents (see for example, Bar-Tal, D., Bar-Tal, Y., Geva, & Yarkin-Levin, in press; Bar-Tal, Y. & Bar-Tal, D. in press). While the first direction usually attempts to reveal the universal principles of knowledge formation, irrespective of specific contents, the second direction frequently focuses on the specific contents that characterize particular individuals or groups. The latter direction is of special importance for understanding these individuals or groups whose knowledge is real for themselves and reflects their understanding of the world. A grasp of this understanding allows one to unravel the cognitive bases of their behavior.

This book concerns the contents of knowledge (i.e., beliefs), specifically of beliefs that are shared by group members. Thus, a belief as a unit of knowledge is an especially important concept for the present analysis. Therefore, the next part of this chapter will describe and elaborate on the nature of beliefs.

Meaning of Beliefs

A belief, as a unit of knowledge, is often labeled as an idea, cognition, thought, or opinion. As indicated before, the contents of beliefs are of an unlimited scope. They may refer to any object, attribute, or relationship between them in varying levels of complexity. Beliefs are held by individuals; their contents, however, are not only significant for themselves as individuals, but also for groups in which they are members.

The Study of Beliefs

Psychologists, sociologists, anthropologists, historians, and political scientists use and study the term *belief*. Surprisingly, the uses of the term by these groups do not differ substantially, although there are some differences in the definitions, conceptualizations, and methods of investigation.

Two major directions in the study of beliefs can be identified. In one direction, beliefs have been examined in their totality. The study of beliefs in their totality has attempted to depict the total set of an individuals' beliefs. This direction has also used alternative terms such as cognition, knowledge, or cognitive map. In the second direction, specific categories of beliefs have been studied. Behavioral scientists have had a long-term interest in such concepts as goals, values, ideology, norms, attributions, intentions, or expectations, which are subcategories of beliefs. In this direction, the interests focus on the contribution of the specific category of beliefs to the understanding of human behavior.

In principle, the study of beliefs either as a totality or in their subcategories can be classified into four areas: (a) acquisition and change of beliefs, (b) structure of beliefs, (c) effects of beliefs, and (d) contents of beliefs. The first area calls attention to the intrapersonal, interpersonal, intragroup, or intergroup process through which beliefs are acquired or changed, and various factors and conditions that influence these processes. The second area concentrates on the modes in which the beliefs are represented, stored, and organized in the mind. The third area focuses on the effects that beliefs have on individuals' and groups' behavior and affect. The fourth area concerns various specific contents of beliefs that an individual or group may have.

Social psychologists, who pay special attention to the study of an individual's cognitive repertoire, have devoted much effort to the examination of human beliefs. The coming pages will review some of the beliefs' conceptions that pertain to their definition, classification, origin, and characterization. These conceptions mainly illustrate the way social psychologists have approached the study of beliefs.

Beliefs have been viewed by social psychologists as units of cognition. They constitute the totality of an individual's knowledge, including what people consider as facts, opinions, or hypotheses, as well as faith. Accordingly, any content can be the subject of a belief. Along this line, Krech and Crutchfield (1948) defined a belief as "an enduring organization of perceptions and cognitions about some aspect of the individual's world" (p. 150). Katz (1960) defined a belief as a description and perception of an object, its characteristics, and its relationship to other objects. Rokeach and Rothman (1965) viewed a belief as a combination of a subject with characterization. Later, as one classification possibility, Rokeach (1968) distinguished among three types of beliefs: descriptive or existential beliefs, which indicate truth or falsity; evaluative beliefs, which judge whether the object of belief is good or bad; and prescriptive or proscriptive beliefs, which judge whether some means or ends of action are desirable or undesirable.

Another social psychologist, Bem (1970), suggested that "if a man perceives some relationship between two things or between something and a characteristic of it, he is said to hold a belief" (p.4). He differentiated between basic beliefs, which are based either on one's own sensory experience or on external authority, and higher order beliefs, which are based on premises. The former beliefs, called primitive, are either products of direct experience with the environment or acquired from external authority. The latter beliefs are formed by inferences from primitive beliefs.

More recently, an extensive analysis of beliefs was provided by Fishbein and Ajzen (1975). They defined a belief as a person's subjective probability judgment concerning "a relation between the object of the belief and some other object, value, concept, or attribute" (p. 131). Thus, a belief that links an object to some attribute represents information about the object. The strength of a belief depends on the ascribed likelihood that the object has the attribute in question. Like Bem (1970), Fishbein and Ajzen differentiated beliefs on the basis of the ways in which they are formed: (a) Descriptive beliefs are formed on the basis of direct experience. They are derived from perception. Through the senses individuals absorb information that serves as a basis for these types of beliefs. (b) Inferential beliefs go beyond the directly observable events and are based on rules of logic that allow inferences. They are formed through thinking that is based on stored beliefs collected in the past. (c) Informational beliefs are formed on the basis of information provided by outside sources such as other individuals, books, television, radio, newspapers, or magazines.

Other behavioral scientists have either accepted the psychological definition of a belief of have adapted the concept for the specific objective of their discipline. For example, Holsti (1962), a political scientist, using Miller, Galanter, and Pribram's (1960) definition, proposed that an individual's belief system is composed of images and constitutes the total knowledge of that individual about the world. Wilker and Milbrath (1970) based their view of a belief system on Kurt Lewin's field theory. According to their approach, an individual's belief system reflects the psychological field defined as a perceptual space. A belief system can include only those elements of which individuals are aware. In this vein, sociologists Borhek and Curtis (1975) defined a belief system as "a set of related ideas (learned and shared), which has some permanence, and to which individuals and/or group exhibit some commitment" (p. 5).

As examples of the specific beliefs category that deals with particular contents, George (1969) reintroduced an "operational code" concept that refers to beliefs about politics that are divided into "instrumental beliefs" and "philosophical beliefs." The former refer to contents about ends-means relationships in the context of political action, and the latter refer to such general contents of human life as "the foundation nature of politics, the nature of political conflict, the role of the individual in history, etc." (p. 199). Similarly, Axelrod (1976) uses the term "cognitive map" to describe a set of conceptual and causal assertions with respect to a particular policy domain. The conceptual assertions are objects in a person's world (e.g., tax rates, national security, or population size), and causal assertions are regarded as relationships between concepts. Perceived combinations and changes in concepts affect the thought calculus of the individual because he or she links different concepts together through complex networks of causal beliefs.

Present Approach to Beliefs

The present conception of a belief, while based on the lay epistemological theory proposed by Kruglanski (1980, 1989), is aligned with the previously described social psychological definitions. Belief is defined as *a proposition to which a person attributes at least a minimal degree of confidence.* A proposition, as a statement about an object(s) or relations between objects and/or attributes, can be of any content. The minimal degree of confidence refers to the likelihood of the proposition to be true from the person's perspective. Individuals hold beliefs for which they have at least minimal confidence in their truth. From a cognitive perspective, beliefs can be viewed as cognitions, since they are units that represent one's reality. They are encoded, stored, and retrieved.

The contents of the propositions can refer to one concept or to several concepts and the relationships among them. "This is a chair," "Here is John," or "It is fast" are examples of simple one-concept propositions, while "I am a patriot," "We are a group," "He loves her," or "Iran is at war with Iraq" are examples of more complex propositions. Obviously, the complexity of the propositions may vary, and therefore beliefs can also have contents such as: "The wrath of those societies in which the capitalist mode of production prevails, presents itself as an immense accumulation of commodities, its unit being a single commodity" (Marx, 1967, p. 35); or "Then temperance is not quietness, nor is the temperate life quiet, upon this view; for the life which is temperate is supposed to be the good" (Plato, 1899, p. 13); or "The transformation of object-libido into narcissistic libido which thus takes place obviously implies an abandonment of sexual aims, a desexualization—a kind of sublimation, therefore" (Freud, 1961, p. 30).

Propositions can be formulated as either affirmative statements (e.g., "She helps me," "War is destructive," or "Brutus probably killed Caesar") or negative statements (e.g., "She does not help me," "War is not destructive," or "Brutus probably did not kill Caesar"). Both types of propositions can be considered as beliefs and individuals may have minimum or maximum confidence in them.

The definition suggested in this chapter is broad and general. It does not differentiate, as philosophers do, between true and untrue beliefs. As indicated, according to the present approach, the totality of a person's beliefs constitutes his/her total knowledge. Also, a belief, as a broad fundamental concept, often has been used for an analysis of different psychological terms. For example, some psychologists have suggested defining attitudes in relation to beliefs. Jones and Gerard (1967) proposed to view an attitude "as the implication of combining a belief with a relevant value" (p. 159). Similarly, Fishbein (1963) suggested that an attitude toward an object can be estimated as a function of beliefs and their evaluative aspects toward that object. In the same way, those psychologists who defined motivation as a goal-orientation desire (e.g., Kagan, 1972) imply that a belief is an important part of the definition, because a goal, as a category of belief, denotes "a cognitive representation of an event in the future that the person believes will permit him to feel better" (Kagan, 1972, p. 54). Another motivation model uses different types of beliefs. Weiner's (1986) cognitive model of motivation focuses on the beliefs of causality as mediators between beliefs' antecedents and behavior.

Characteristics of Beliefs

Psychologists have suggested different features and dimensions to characterize beliefs. It is interesting therefore to review their scope and variety as a background for describing characteristics that are important for the present conception. In one of the earlier conceptions, Krech and Crutchfield (1948) proposed the following seven characteristics to describe beliefs: kind, content, precision, specificity, strength, importance, and verifiability. Differences in kind refer to the various categories to which beliefs can be classified (e.g., beliefs about art, philosophy, God). The contents refer to specific topics that are the subjects of beliefs (e.g., "It is good to be a group member," or "I dislike large groups"). Precision describes a belief's clarity and differentiation from other beliefs. While some beliefs are clear, explicit, and differentiated, others are vague, confused, and undifferentiated. Specificity refers to the relations among sets of beliefs. While some beliefs stand virtually alone, others are related to different sets of beliefs. Strength describes the persistence of beliefs a long time. While some beliefs are resistant to change, others are temporary and easily changed. Importance describes the extent to which a belief accounts for a person's behavior. Some beliefs are important to individuals' daily behavior, while other beliefs are not. Verifiability refers to the degree a given belief can be proven. This characteristic reflects a subjective conception of what is proven and what is not proven.

Rokeach, who has spent much of his career studying beliefs, proposed three major dimensions to characterize belief systems (Rokeach, 1960). The first dimension differentiates between belief and disbelief systems. According to Rokeach "the *belief system* is conceived to represent all the beliefs, sets, expectancies, or hypotheses, conscious and unconscious, that a person at a given time accepts as true of the world he lives in." The disbelief system contains those beliefs that, "to one degree or another, a person at a given time rejects as false" (p. 33). This dimension can be further differentiated on the basis of degrees of isolation and differentiation. The former property describes the degree to which beliefs are related to each other and the latter describes the richness of details. The second dimension, central-peripheral dimension, refers to the contents and sources of beliefs. Central beliefs are about the nature of the physical world, the nature of self, and the generalized other; intermediate beliefs pertain to authorities; and the peripheral beliefs are those beliefs that are derived from authority. The third dimension describes a person's reference to time. Some beliefs contain a broad perspective of time consisting of past, present, and future, while other beliefs focus on one time without presenting the continuity from past to future. In his later writing, Rokeach (1973) elaborated the second dimension, suggesting that the more central a belief, the more it will resist change and the more it is connected to other beliefs. Central beliefs are mostly derived from a personal encounter with the object of a belief and are supported by unanimous social consensus.

According to Bem (1970) it is possible to characterize beliefs with three features that pertain to interrelationships among beliefs:

(1) The degree to which they are differentiated (vertical structure), which means the extent to which they are based on a long chain of syllogistic reasoning, or in other

words, the extent to which they are based on quasi-logical inference. An example of such an inference is, "Smoking causes cancer. Cancer can cause death. Therefore, smokers die younger than nonsmokers" (p. 11);

(2) The extent to which they are broadly based (horizontal structure), which depends on the number of syllogistic chains of reasoning that lead to the same belief (i.e., a number of propositions that lead to a conclusion). A conclusion, "Smokers die younger," based on several propositions such as "Smoking causes cancer," "Smokers drink more heavily than nonsmokers," and "Smokers are more prone to have heart disease," is an example of horizontal structure;

(3) The degree of centrality, which describes their effects on other beliefs. A change of a central belief leads to alteration of many other beliefs, while a change of peripheral beliefs does not affect other beliefs.

Although it is probably possible to think about additional characteristics, the review described the ones most used by social psychologists. The suggested characteristics have to be evaluated for their use in explaining human reactions. They cannot serve only a descriptive purpose, but must also serve as a contributing factor to understanding differentiating behavior of individuals and groups.

The present approach focuses on four features: confidence, centrality, interrelationship, and functionality. These features, which characterize beliefs of an individual as well as of a group, are relevant to the conceptual framework to be proposed later. They are used through the analysis and are essential for the analysis of group behavior.

Confidence

As implied by the definition, beliefs differ in the extent to which a person has confidence in them (Kruglanski, 1989). The dimension of confidence indicates that a person may have a minimum confidence in some beliefs, and therefore these beliefs are considered as hypotheses, possibilities, or uncertainties. In other beliefs, a person may have full confidence, and therefore these beliefs are considered as facts, truths, or verities. The former beliefs will be expressed using "possibly" or "maybe," while the latter are stated in definite ways. Between the two extremes of minimum confidence and full confidence are various degrees of confidence on which different beliefs can be placed. Thus, for example, a person may be absolutely confident that he observed an accident, that Columbus discovered America in 1492, that his father is a smart person, or that democracy is the best political system; but at the same time he may be doubtful about whether he saw a flower in a garden, whether the Earth was created by God, whether his friend is a nice person, or whether justice can be achieved in any political system. People can be confident, or doubtful, in any content of beliefs. Also, there may be various reasons and causes for an individual's high or low confidence in a given belief. Confidence reflects a subjective state of mind that does not necessarily relate to any specific ways of verification or proof.

Centrality

Another dimension that differentiates beliefs is centrality. *The degree of a belief's centrality is expressed by the frequency with which the belief is accessible in the cognitive system and the extent to which it is relevant for a wide range of evaluations, decisions, or judgments, including behaviors* (Bar-Tal, D., 1986). That is, central beliefs are often accessible in the cognitive system and are frequently taken into consideration when individuals make inferences about other issues, including decisions to perform various behaviors. (This definition differs from other conceptions of centrality.) The first condition reflects how often people think about the given belief, since accessibility indicates the readiness with which a stored belief is recovered from memory (Higgins & King, 1981). The second condition reflects how often the belief is utilized in various cognitive processes of knowledge formation (e.g., decision making or impression formation), since individuals utilize beliefs that are relevant to the specific epistemic question that they are entertaining (Wyer & Srull, 1986).

Of the beliefs that an individual has, some are central while others are less central. The least central, peripheral beliefs are almost never accessible and almost never taken into consideration when a person makes evaluations or decisions. They are available in the cognitive system, but they are rarely recalled. This does not mean that peripheral beliefs cannot be important at certain times. Peripheral beliefs may be accessible and influential in specific judgments, while the centrality feature, like other features, reflects a characterization that lasts over time. Central beliefs are often accessible and relevant in various inferences. However, it should not be implied that central beliefs are constantly accessible or that their centrality lasts forever. With time, central beliefs may move into periphery.

An example of central beliefs may be such thoughts as "I am an Israeli," "A Ph.D. degree is crucial for life success," "I love this person," or "Exercising may keep me young" (see Bar-Tal, D., 1989a; Bar-Tal, D., & Antebi, 1989 for specific examples). It means that these beliefs are frequently accessible and relevant to inferences and decision making that people holding them make. Any content of a belief may be central, and individuals and groups differ with regard to contents that are central in their system.

Interrelationship

In principle, systems of beliefs are coherent, organized structures. This means that beliefs do not normally exist in isolation from one another, but are related to each other, forming systems. Nevertheless, beliefs differ in the extent to which they are related. Thus, while some beliefs are interrelated into large systems, others are interrelated into small systems. Some may even be isolated—not related to any other beliefs. This characteristic has been of special interest for political scientists and sociologists (e.g., Converse, 1964; Dawson, 1979; Jaros & Grant, 1974; Lane, 1973). For example, Converse views a set of interrelated beliefs as a belief system, which he defines as "a configuration of ideas and attitudes in which the elements are bound together by some form of constraint or functional interdependence" (p. 207). The systems differ with regard to a range of objects that "are referents for the ideas and attitudes in the system" (p. 208). People differ with regard to the extent to which they construct their beliefs into systems. The most important claim by Converse is that the political beliefs of many individuals, especially of the less educated, are not organized into systems. Obviously, the degree of interrelationship may vary from individual to individual, but can also vary from domain to domain. Individuals may have interrelated beliefs in some domains, but not in others (see Bar-Tal, 1989a, for example). Thus, for example, a person's beliefs about consumer behavior may be related to beliefs about the economic and political systems. But at the same time, two or three beliefs about the Arctic Sea may be isolated.

Functionality

Beliefs differ with regard to the functions that they fulfill. The idea that beliefs fulfill various functions for the needs of different people is not a new one. Years ago, social psychologists proposed functional theories of beliefs and attitudes. Krech and Crutchfield (1948) were among the first social psychologists who pointed out the functional significance of beliefs and attitudes. They suggested that the fundamental function of beliefs is to provide a meaningful structure of the world, but that beliefs also serve other needs that arise in response to various situations. Smith (1968), who propagated the functional view of knowledge, suggested that "a person acquires and maintains attitudes and other learned psychological structures to the extent that they are useful to him in his inner economy of adjustment and his outer economy of adaptation" (p. 86). Rokeach (1960) suggested two major functions of beliefs. According to him "all belief-disbelief systems serve two powerful and conflicting sets of motives at the same time: the need for a cognitive framework to know and to understand, and the need to ward off threatening aspects of reality" (p. 67).

Adorno, Frenkel-Brunswik, Levinson, and Sanford (1950) provided one of the early elaborated psychological conceptions of beliefs, in which they suggested that the political, economical, and social beliefs of an individual often form a broad coherent system that expresses the deep, underlying needs of that individual's personality. In their study, these psychologists focused on anti-Semitic and fascistic beliefs. They found that these beliefs serve needs of inner structure. In a similar direction, a number of studies have shown that political beliefs serve psychological needs. That is, political beliefs are functional to various psychological needs. Therefore, individuals with certain psychological characteristics may hold certain political beliefs (see a collection of articles by DiRenzo, 1974).

Sarnoff (1960) suggested that attitudes play a functional role in reducing tension aroused as a result of activated motives. Specifically, he suggested that individuals develop their attitudes in the process of tension reduction. "An individual's attitude toward a class of objects is determined by the particular role these objects have come to play in facilitating responses which reduce the tension of particular motives and which resolve particular conflicts among motives" (p. 261).

Smith, Bruner, and White (1956), who attempted to relate concepts of attitudes and opinions to personality, proposed three functions that these concepts serve for individuals:

1. *objects appraisal function*, which refers to the usefulness of orienting individuals in the environment, since opinions and/or attitudes allow classification of objects and raise intentions to behave;

2. *social adjustment function*, which refers to facilitation, maintenance, and disruption of social relationships, since attitudes help individuals either to be accepted into a group or to maintain their independence from the group; and

3. *externalization function*, which refers to ego protection from anxiety generated by inner problems, since opinions and/or attitudes allow individuals to externalize various problems.

One of the proponents of the functional theory of attitudes is Daniel Katz, who suggested that "the functional approach is the attempt to understand the reasons people hold the attitudes they do. The reasons, however, are at the level of psychological motivations and not at the accidents of external events and circumstances" (Katz, 1960, p. 170). Katz proposed the four following functions that attitudes may serve:

1. *The instrumental, adjustive, or utilitarian function*, which refers to satisfaction of needs. Individuals hold attitudes in order to get rewards and avoid punishments.

2. *The ego defensive function*, which refers to protection from threats or unacceptable impulses. Individuals hold attitudes in order to protect their egos from unacceptable information about self and certain realities in the external world.

3. *The value expressive function*, which refers to the positive expression of one's central values. Individuals hold attitudes that express personal values and are important for the self-concept.

4. *The knowledge function*, which refers to an adequate structure of everything individuals know. People hold attitudes since attitudes provide meaning, understanding, and organization of their world.

These functions correspond to the ones proposed by Smith et al. (1956).

Beliefs are not only functional for individuals as unique entities, but also for groups as a whole. Groups as social structures have various needs that are fulfilled by beliefs held by group members. For example, Lane (1973) suggested that it is possible to distinguish between internal and external group functions: "The internal functions served by belief systems are those of interpretation, coordination, morale building, leadership legitimization, defining equity and justice within the system, and providing formulas for conflict resolution" (p. 96). The external functions delineate the location and limits of the group. That is, the belief system enables the formulation of social identity, which is "a sense of group placement, of allies, of people like me; in contrast to strangers and enemies" (p. 97).

While the most salient function of beliefs is the organization of the world in a meaningful way, which allows an understanding or a feeling of knowing, other needs, such as the need to maintain a positive self-image, the need of security, the need of justice, the need to be free of limitations, the need to be socially accepted, or the need to avoid threats, may also underlie various beliefs. The list of individuals' and groups' needs that behavioral scientists have proposed is long and probably not entirely exhaustive. Individuals and groups differ with regard to their beliefs and needs. In addition, the same beliefs may serve different needs and the same need can be reflected in different beliefs. The relations between beliefs and needs vary from individual to individual and also may change from time to time within the same person. Functionality of beliefs has been suggested to be a very important characteristic. It plays a determinative role in beliefs' change (see, for example, Bar-Tal, D., 1989a; Bar-Tal, D., Kruglanski, & Klar, 1989).

In sum, as already indicated, the described characteristics of beliefs are not stable. They may change from time to time, or from situation to situation. This is not to say that they necessarily have to change, but the conception suggests a fluid structure of beliefs and their characteristics. It is recognized that the belief system is dynamic. Changes take place continuously. However, changes are dependent on various factors, such as a belief's structure, a person's cognitive abilities and motivation, and availability of information. Beliefs that were considered as facts can change and become hypotheses. Beliefs may even disappear from the cognitive repertoire, since the individual may lose minimum confidence in them and substitute them with others. Beliefs such as "China is the United States' enemy," "The New York Stock market will not crash in 1987," or "The sun surrounds the earth" are only a few examples of the above described changes. Obviously, a change may occur in the opposite direction as well. Beliefs that were never in the cognitive repertoire may become *absolute truth*, and past *hypotheses* may turn into *facts*. "Smoking causes cancer," "It is possible to fly over the Atlantic" or "Egypt and Israel will sign a peace agreement" are examples of changes in this direction. Also, beliefs that were obscure may become central (e.g., "AIDS is transferred through sexual relations"), and beliefs that were central may almost never become accessible again (e.g., "Japan is at war with us").

Finally, it should be stressed that even when individuals hold the same beliefs, the beliefs' characteristics may differ. The different experiences that individuals have, their different cognitive abilities, and motivations are responsible to a large extent for these individual differences. However, groups of individuals do hold the same beliefs characterized in the same way. As proposed, human beings who live in groups go through similar patterns of socialization, receive the same information, and often have the same or similar experiences. Thus, it is not surprising that members of the same group, and even members of different groups, also share the same beliefs. It is the focus of this book to discuss those beliefs that are shared by group members and considered by them to characterize their group.

Summary

This chapter outlines the epistemological foundations for the present belief conception. The conception draws its basis from the nonjustificational approach to science, which suggests that all human beliefs are uncertain and conjectural. Their verification depends on the theories held by individuals; therefore, scientists, as all other persons, can not only focus on the limited features of their environment, but can also examine the rationality of scientific propositions only by testing the consistency between the newly formed idea, or collected observation, and the held knowledge.

In this framework, beliefs, viewed as units of knowledge, are defined as propositions to which a person attributes at least a minimal degree of confidence. There are many characteristics of beliefs, but the ones that are of special importance for the present analysis are: confidence, centrality, interrelationship, and functionality. Confidence differentiates beliefs on the basis of truth attributed to them; centrality characterizes the extent of beliefs' accessibility in individuals' repertoire and their use in various considerations that individuals make; interrelationship indicates the extent to which the belief is related to other beliefs; functionality differentiates beliefs on the basis of the needs that they fulfill.

In general, beliefs are of unlimited contents, are held by different individuals who attribute even to the same belief different levels of truth, change in the degree of the truth ascribed to them, and are organized along with interrelated beliefs into systems. The study of beliefs is one of the focuses of social scientists, especially social psychologists, who have devoted much effort to studying acquisition and change of beliefs, their structure, their contents, and their effects mainly on individuals' affect and behavior. This is so, because individuals, not groups, hold beliefs, although group members share the same beliefs.

In the past, the study of shared beliefs preoccupied social scientists. Therefore, before turning to the present conception, which deals with shared beliefs that characterize a group, a short historical review of the preoccupation with shared beliefs in the early days of behavioral sciences is presented. This review provides an historical perspective for the framework later suggested.

Chapter 2

Historical Perspective on Shared Beliefs

Although today's psychological textbooks do not deal with cognitive commonality and shared beliefs, the early days of social psychology were marked by extensive preoccupation with the cognitive activity of groups. From the end of the previous century through the beginning of the present one, concepts such as *group mind*, *collective unconscious*, or *collective representations* were introduced and used. This trend reflects the predominant preoccupation with group behavior that characterized the early days of social psychology.

It is therefore important to review the forgotten work of the behavioral scientists who, in the early days of sociology and psychology, laid the basis for studying group behavior. Their contributions about the cognitive products of groups have been relatively disregarded, although few behavioral scientists would deny the existence of shared group beliefs and their influence on group behavior. The present review aims to reintroduce old ideas and critically evaluate them.

Allport (1954, 1968, 1985), in his historical analysis of the social psychological origins, devoted special attention to the different conceptions of a "common manner of thinking, feeling, and willing," which served as a basis for understanding group behavior. He identified seven different approaches, which appeared with the emergence of social psychology:

1. *Analogical doctrines* compare the holistic characteristics of human society to other systems, such as human organisms or modern mechanics (e.g., Spencer, 1900; Wiener, 1948). In this view, individuals are replaceable, but the common mental content and functioning of society continue as long as society subsists.
2. *The collective unconscious approach* suggests that the subconscious mental life is extended beyond personal experiences to collective representations in the collective unconscious (e.g., James, 1902; Jung, 1922).
3. *The objective mind approach* views society as having its own consciousness (e.g., goals, pleasures) beyond that of the individuals, who are only agents of the group (e.g., Green, 1900).

4. *Folk psychology* maintains that individuals living in the same society develop common culture in the form of similar ideas as expressed in art, morality, law, folklore, etc. (e.g., Judd, 1926; Wundt, 1916).
5. *Cultural determinism*, a somewhat similar approach, focuses on common cultural factors as the determinants of human behavior (e.g., White, 1949).
6. *Collective representations* proposes that individuals, because of their association, form collective thoughts and behaviors that exist independently of any single person. These collective representations are beyond personal consciousness (e.g., Durkheim, 1898).
7. *The common and reciprocal segments of behavior approach* indicates that social institutions are abstractions of the behavior and consciousness of individuals (e.g., McDougall, 1920).

Within the framework of this approach, McDougall suggested the concept *group mind*, which indicates that highly organized human societies acquire an organized system of mental or purposive forces that are largely independent of the qualities of the group members. This concept received much attention and stirred up considerable controversy. It has become a frame of reference for any conception that mentions group cognitive activity or group ideas.

The present analysis classifies the various contributions to group cognitive activities, which appeared with the emergence of psychology, into two categories. One category consists of conceptions that viewed the formation and existence of a group's mental products as independent of individuals who constitute the group. The other category consists of contributions that suggested that a group's mental products are formed, shared, and bound to the influence processes within the group. The first category views the contents of common beliefs as predetermined and independent of the wills or desires of group members, whereas the second category considers belief contents to be affected by the social processes of the individuals who constitute the group. Thus, the differentiating criterion is whether beliefs shared by group members have a superindividual integrity, irrespective of what the specific individuals who comprise the group do, or whether the shared beliefs are the products of continuous social influence processes through which the contents of beliefs and the extent of dissemination are determined.

The Superindividual Integrity of Common Beliefs

In the first category of contributions, we find the works of Jung, Wundt, Le Bon, Freud, and Judd.

Jung's Collective Unconscious

One of the most extreme examples of the superindividual existence of common beliefs is provided by Jung (1922, 1959, 1983). According to Jung (1959), societies, groups, and even mankind in general have *collective representations* or *mystical collective ideas*, which include such topics as religion, justice, and feelings. Collective representations are part of conscious awareness of human beings. But Jung directed his attention to the *collective unconscious*, which individuals carry in addition to personal unconscious:

> In addition to our immediate consciousness, which is of a thoroughly personal nature and which we believe to be the only empirical psyche (even if we tack on the personal unconscious as an appendix), there exists a second psychic system of a collective, universal, and impersonal nature which is identical in all individuals. This collective unconscious is not developed individually but is inherited. It consists of pre-existing forms, the archetypes, which can only become conscious secondarily and which can give definite form to certain psychic contents. [Jung, 1959, p. 3]

Collective unconscious is at a deeper level than personal unconscious. It consists of mythological motifs or primordial images, which Jung called *archetypes*. Archetypes appear in every human being's dreams, fantasies, or even conscious representations, and are expressed in symbolic figures, myths, or fairy tales.

In a detailed analysis, Jung (1959) suggested that the mind—through its physical counterpart, the brain—inherits certain characteristics that determine the experiences that a person has and how he/she reacts to them. To some extent, these characteristics are linked with the past of the human species and evolved in the organic evolution. The collective unconscious was formed in the past, and its contents have never been conscious within the lifetime of the individual; human beings inherited these contents (primordial images) from their ancestral past. This is so because psychologically, the group precedes the existence of the individual and is more powerful than any of the members who compose it. The group imposed on individuals the collective psyche—the collective unconscious.

The inherited images are predispositions for experiencing and responding to the world in the same way one's ancestors did. Examples of these images are the fear of snakes and the fear of darkness. However, the development and expression of such predispositions depend entirely upon the individual's experiences. But, the contents of the collective unconscious are responsible for the selectivity of perception and action. Individuals easily perceive some things and react to them in certain ways because the collective unconscious is predisposed to them.

Wundt's Folk Soul

Wundt's (1916) concept of *folk soul* refers to "those mental products that are created by a community of human life and are, therefore, inexplicable in terms merely of individual consciousness, since they presuppose the reciprocal action of many" (p. 3). Folk souls, which consist of language, religion, mythology, and customs, are products of a culture. Each group, whether a local community, tribe, or nation, develops through reciprocal activity collective mental products, the folk souls. The child, with the development of his/her own consciousness, absorbs folk souls related to the mental products of the community. However, in the same way that individuals synthesize all of their psychic compounds, so does the community or the folk. This process is beyond the individual psyche. According to Wundt, just as the psyche of the individual is built up in the form of a progression of superimposed syntheses, the folk soul is also a synthesis of syntheses. It consists of something creatively new, beyond the sum of its elements, that is not equal to the sum of the individuals of which the folk is composed.

In this meaning, the concept *folk soul* refers to the superindividual psychic experience, in the same way that the individual soul refers to that of the psychic experience of the individual. The folk soul is a superindividual synthesis that transcends the scope of individual consciousness. Thus, folk souls are as real as the psychic life of the individuals.

Le Bons' Collective Mind

Le Bon (1968) was interested in crowd behavior and therefore analyzed specific collective behavior. Nevertheless, his analysis also refers to group behavior in a specific, face-to-face situation. Because he focused on the cognitive activities that take place in this situation, it is interesting to review the description.

Le Bon (1968) viewed a *crowd* as a specific concept to denote gathering of individuals for a certain purpose. Such a gathering also constitutes a psychologically organized group whose members are in one place. The psychological crowd is characterized by the formation of a *collective mind*. "The sentiments and ideas of all the persons in the gathering take one and the same direction, and their conscious personality vanishes" (p. 2). This means that

> whoever be the individuals that compose it, however like or unlike be their mode of life, their occupations, their character, or their intelligence, the fact that they are transformed into a crowd puts them in possession of a sort of collective mind which makes them, feel, think, and act in manner quite different from that in which each individual of them feel, think, and act were he in a state of isolation. (p. 6)

This conception implies a mental unity of a mass, which is defined by the uniformity of ideas and feelings.

Specifically, Le Bon compares the state of individuals in a crowd with the hypnosis state. They lose their own unique and independent personalities, bending in the direction of contagious and common behavior, guided by unconscious motives, driven by emotional and instinctual impulses. In these situations, the group has complete power over the individual, who succumbs to group impulses: "His ideas and feelings have undergone a transformation, and the transformation is so profound as to change the miser into a spendthrift" (p. 13). In these situations, individuals think and do things that would be unthinkable when in isolation. They gain new qualities. The crowd returns to primitivism and to intellectual inferiority by reasoning through images, being driven by emotions, and being motivated by instincts.

Freud's Group Psychology

Freud's book *Group Psychology and the Analysis of the Ego* (1960) is one of the early systematic analyses of group behavior. Drawing upon the ideas of Le Bon and

McDougall and using his own concepts from individual psychology, Freud recognized that an individual, "as a member of a race, of a nation, of a caste, of a profession, of an institution, or a component part of a crowd," behaves differently from individuals in isolation. In a group, social anxiety, which is the essence of conscience, disappears; as a result, all that has been repressed can uninhibitedly appear in behavior.

Freud accepted Le Bon's comparison of the individual's behavior in a group to hypnotic influence, but in contrast to Le Bon, Freud did not think that individuals exhibit new special qualities in group behavior. According to him, individuals in group situations free themselves from their inhibitions. "When individuals come together in a group all their individual inhibitions fall away and all the cruel, brutal and destructive instincts, which lie dormant in individuals as relics of a primitive epoch are stirred up to find free gratification" (p. 15). However, according to Freud, groups are also capable of unselfishness and devotion to an ideal. Moral behavior of group members can be improved, but intellectual behavior cannot. Groups demand illusions, not truth. Their behavior depends on leaders, since groups have a need for leaders and a thirst for obedience.

Following McDougall, Freud accepts the notion that highly organized groups develop collective mental lives. However, he suggests that it takes place as a result of the members' effort to "equip the group with the attributes of the individual" in order to make the group unique and distinctive. Freud proposed that the underlying basis for the mental changes is libido, the energy that expresses love. The libido holds the group together and serves as a basis for its behavior.

But this type of object-cathexis, based on sexuality, is not the only kind of emotional tie in a group. Identifications between group members, and between the leader and members, are also possible. The process of identification is essential for group formation. It implies that group members put "one and the same object in the place of their ego ideal and have consequently identified themselves with one another in their ego" (p. 47). This process provides the bond for group relations.

Judd's Social Consciousness

Judd (1926), while recognizing the individual's personal tendencies, focused especially on the common products of group members' activity called *social consciousness*. Social consciousness, which is always a result of group action, is expressed through common social institutions. Institutions reflect a cooperative effort of group members. They exist beyond the specific individuals and characterize a particular group by reflecting, for example, its language or government. If one needs the definition of a social group, "one may think of it as a collection of human individuals which is capable of setting up an institution. A group can effectively establish its institutions only on the basis of its consciousness and will. The institutions are as manifold as the needs of the group cooperation" (p. 76). Through careful guidance by adults, children develop social consciousness. Group members are pressed to conform to customs and practices implied by the social consciousness. Thus individuals behave according to customs and practices not originated by them.

Judd believed that the ability to create social consciousness is a great achievement of the human race. This achievement made human evolution unique:

> ... the accumulation of experience from generation to generation through social institutions has brought into the world a new order of reality. Institutions are crystallized ideas. They make possible the transmission of ideas. They are detached from the minds in which they originated and are capable of affecting other minds. (p. 17)

Common Beliefs as Products of Group Members

This category treats common beliefs as products of social processes within the group. Group members form and change their shared beliefs. In this category we find works of McDougall, Durkheim, Thomas, Tarde, and Bekhterev.

McDougall's Group Mind

McDougall's (1920) conception of *group mind* has received special prominence in social psychology partly because he is considered as one of the first professed social psychologists, and partly because of the controversy that followed the publication of the idea (see Allport, 1924a). As a result of the limelight and the controversy, McDougall (1939) revised and clarified his conception of group mind in a way that moved it more toward the second category of the present classification.

First, in his book entitled *Group Mind*, McDougall (1920) suggested dealing with groups as single entities that have a group mind. This is based on an assumption that "when a number of men think and feel and act together, the mental operations are apt to be very different from those he would achieve if he faced the situation as an isolated individual" (p. 31). These mental collective operations appear when there is a common object of mental activity, a common way of feeling about the object, and some degree of reciprocal influence among the group members.

His arguments for treating the group as an entity with a mind rested on the following premises:

1. A group preserves characteristic behavioral habits and structure despite the continual replacement of actual individuals.
2. A group shows memory for group experiences and learning.
3. A group is capable of responding as a whole to stimuli directed to its parts. (By acting as a group it solves problems of individuals and subgroups.)
4. A group possesses drives that become integrated in group functions.
5. A group experiences moods of expansiveness, depression, and pugnacity, which influence its behavior.
6. A group shows collective deliberation and collective volition.
7. A group exercises some degree of choice about the admission or rejection of those who aggregate toward it.

To propose the concept of group mind was peculiar, since McDougall explicitly pointed out that it is not a collective conscious or unconscious, but rather a system of relations between the social minds of group members. The concept of group mind refers to the continuity and existence of the group despite turnover of the membership. It corresponds to the idea of shared sentiments, thoughts, and traditions. It "consists of the same stuff as individual minds ... but the parts in the several individual minds reciprocally imply and complement one another and together make up the system which consists wholly of them" (p. 11).

McDougall recognized that group mind does not exist over and above the minds of the group members. It "only exists in the minds of the members." But, he argues, it exists "over and above any sum of those minds created by mere addition" (p. 26). He suggested five conditions for high-level mental life:

1. some degree of continuity of group existence;
2. an idea of the wholeness of the group;
3. intergroup relations that foster group identity;
4. common knowledge of traditions, customs, and habits; and
5. organization of the group through interlocking roles.

In the 1939 publication of his book, McDougall clarified his position, directing it toward a second category of conceptions. He proposed that the concept group mind expresses the Gestaltist notion that the whole is more than the sum of its parts and that the understanding of the whole requires laws or principles that cannot be arrived at by the study of the parts alone. This view

> recognizes the organization of the group mind as consisting in the similarities of the structure of the individual minds (similarities that render them capable of responding in similar fashion to the common features of the environment, both social and physical) and in those mutual adaptations of individual minds which render them capable of harmonious cooperation and reciprocal supplementation in their efforts towards the realization of a common goal. (p. xv)

Group mind, which appears in societies that have long life and are highly organized, consists of moral, aesthetic, and intellectual traditions that the society accumulates as it develops and molds the individual mind. "Each member of the group so moulded bears within him some part of the group mind, some socially moulded mental structure that is part of the total structure of the group mind" (p. xvi). In other words, it is an organized system of mental or purposive forces that have tendencies, a power of molding individuals, and a power of perpetuating itself as a self-identical system that gradually changes and has life of its own. This structure is independent of the qualities of the individuals who are its group members. It constitutes a whole system composed of the minds of individuals that reciprocate and complement one another. Thus, group mind exists in the minds of the members as a collective, but does not exist in total in the mind of any one of them.

Durkheim's Collective Representations

Durkheim discusses collectively shared cognitive products labeled as *collective representations*, which consist of "the totality of beliefs and sentiments common to average members of the same society" (Durkheim, 1933, p. 79). This system has its own life. Though it is realized only in individuals, it is a type of psychic society, a type that has its own properties, conditions of existence, and mode of development. Durkheim (1953) suggested that collective representations are the customs, traditions, values, ideas, and other elements of society that take shape historically in human culture and form the milieu in which the individual is socialized and educated. In this respect, they are the perceptions and ideological interpretations of social and cultural phenomena, and serve as the mode of explanation and justification in the society.

Thus, collective representations can be viewed as the emergent products of social life that are shared by participants in a collective. Specifically, although they stem from the substratum brain cells of associated individuals, they can neither be reduced to nor wholly explained by features of individuals: They have sui generis characteristics. In other words, collective representations exist independently of specific individuals. As Durkheim (1953) explained,

> When we said elsewhere that social facts are in a sense independent of individuals and exterior to individual minds, we only affirmed of the social world what we have just established for the psychic world. Society has for its substratum, the mass of associated individuals. The system which they form by uniting together and which varies according to their geographical disposition, and the nature and number of their channels of communication, is the base from which social life is raised. If there is nothing extraordinary in the fact that individual representations, produced by the action and reaction between neural elements, are not inherent in these elements, there is nothing surprising in the fact that collective representations produced by the action and reaction between individual minds that form the society, do not derive directly from the latter and consequently surpass them. (p. 24–25)

Furthermore, according to Durkheim (1933), collective representations have distinctive qualitative features, which differ from individuals' representations. Collective rules enjoy the moral prestige that individuals spontaneously associate with all collectively shared beliefs; because these norms are invariably imposed upon the individual by public opinion, they engender sentiments that are qualitatively different from those evoked by individual representations. As a result, collective norms have an intensity and compelling force that far exceed those of privately formulated rules. Individuals assume that they are derived from and enforced by some power, real or ideal, that is superior to themselves. In this respect, collective representations are sources of legitimization for institutional practices and actual behavior in society. They provide communal identity and similarity, which, in turn, serve as a basis for solidarity (Durkheim, 1951).

Social psychologists are currently actively engaged in pursuing Durkheim's conception of collective representation, which is one of the few past contributions to be revived in the present time. This revival has been accomplished by Moscovici, who introduced the conception of *social representation* on the basis of Durkheim's work (e.g., Farr and Moscovici, 1984; Moscovici, 1961, 1984). However, because Moscovici's conception is greatly influenced by modern social psychology, it is typical of the present approaches of constructionistic knowledge. According to Moscovici (1984), social representations denote shared beliefs, images, and affects that persons in a particular society hold. In other words, they reflect the knowledge that individuals in the particular group acquire and communicate. They "are phenomena which need to be described, and to be explained. They are specific phenomena which are related to a particular mode of understanding and of communicating—a mode which creates both reality and common sense" (Moscovici, 1984, p. 19). In this respect, social representations bridge the gap between individual and societal realities by providing a framework of social, intragroup understanding. On this basis, group members can understand each other and communicate with each other. This view implies that, on the one hand, the knowledge embedded in social representations is dynamic because it may change and/or disappear. On the other hand, however, this knowledge is essential for group functioning, unifying the group or the society and allowing the collective to operate as a system.

Thomas' Definition of the Situation

Thomas (1917, 1951) discussed group cognitive activity from the perspective of the common definition of the group situation. According to Thomas, groups develop their own *definitions of situations*, which reflect their unique view of the world. Group members internalize these definitions through the process of socialization. Only on the basis of agreement between group members regarding the definitions can a social life in a group take place. This is a prerequisite for group functioning. Indeed, in most cases, individuals learn to define situations in group terms so that behavior conforms to social norms. When the agreement between the collective definition ceases, extreme disorganization may occur, which often causes the general decay of all the group institutions.

In the classic analysis of Polish peasants, Thomas and Znaniecki (1958) suggested a framework for understanding group behavior. In their analysis, the concepts of values and attitudes are of special importance. A value is a "social datum" that serves as an object of meaningful and useful activity to members of a social group, such as food, money, or ideas. An attitude is an individual's acquired orientation toward a value, for example, fear, devotion, or hunger. Group members form common attitudes and values as a result of the common conditions in which they live. According to Thomas and Znaniecki, social psychologists study attitudes in relation to historically specific values, especially toward rules—values whose purpose is to regulate the individual's relations to the group. These values are shared and provide the basis for common group activity:

> the field of social psychology practically comprises first of all, the attitudes that are more or less generally found among the members of the social group, have a real importance in the life-organization of the individuals who have developed them, and manifest themselves in the social activities of these individuals. (p. 30)

Tarde's Social Group

According to Tarde (1969), associations among individuals are formed as a result of the formation of bonds. The basis for bonds among group members "lies in their simultaneous conviction or passion and in their awareness of sharing at the same time an idea or a wish with a great number of other men" (p. 278). Thus, groups are formed on the basis of shared beliefs and desires, which constitute social reality for group members and form mental cohesion. "This reality changes by imperceptible nuances, but this does not preclude that from the variants there emerges a collective result which is almost constant" (p. 115).

Tarde did not accept the existence of collective consciousness beyond that of individuals. He suggested that group thoughts (e.g., moral maxims, religious rites) are transferred from one individual to another (mostly from parents, teachers, or peers). The basic process through which the beliefs are transferred among the group members is imitation (Tarde, 1907).

According to Tarde, every group act implies an imitative relationship among group members. This process enables a formation of commonality and sharing the same beliefs and desires. Furthermore, he recognized the importance of mass media (i.e., journalism) for the dissemination of some ideas to large populations. In his opinion, such disseminations allow for the formation of large associations.

Bekhterev's Collective Reflexology*

Bekhterev (1921) tried to introduce objective analysis to the issues of collective actions and reactions without resorting to subjective interpretations. He based this analysis on reflexology, a scientific discipline that he attempted to develop. In his view, it is possible to explain much of collective behavior within the framework of *collective reflexology*. Collective behavior, like individual behavior, is an outcome of specific conditions in the environment and biological bases. In our case, the conditions in the environment pertain to tradition and social standards that provide the framework for social behavior. Thus, collective reflexology can explain "manifestations of correlative activity of a whole group of people and their external responses under certain conditions."

Of special importance for the present review is Bekhterev's concept of *correlative activity* (i.e., neuropsychological activity), which he used in reflexology to describe mental activity, but defined as the sum of higher, or associative, reflexes. (Associative reflexes develop on the basis of common reflexes, which are purely biological.) According to Bekhterev, the group affects individuals' correlative activity through interpersonal communications. In this process, collective correlative activity evolves that is based on unifying elements such as "common mood, joint observation, collective concentration and decision, joint decision making, and shared goals and activity."

The products of collective correlative activity "are based exclusively on individual mental processes," but groups establish mental unity. Group members influence each other and new mental content is added to the individual's repertoire. These additions are common to group members. The final product leads to an "amalgamation" of the mental unity rather than to a formation of "a single collective soul." Nevertheless, the outputs of collective correlative activity reveal characteristics that cannot be found in an individual's private repertoire.

*Special thanks are granted to Lloyd Strickland who directed my attention to Bekhterev's ideas and provided the translations of his work.

Bekhterev pointed out that

> collective activity develops along the same line and according to the same laws as
> individual activity. Therefore, in the activity of every collective and every
> individual we can distinguish hereditary-organic manifestations, greater or lesser
> excitability, collective mood, ability to observe, collective concentration, collective
> creativity and judgment as one of its manifestations, which leads to certain results
> in the form of a decision or a decree and, finally, to the execution of this decision
> or decree in the form of a particular action.

Group behavior, like individual behavior, is based on reflexes. Collective reflexes of
panic, attack, or concentration exemplify basic group behavior. In addition, groups
develop collective associative reflexes that are based on the substitution of a real
stimulus by a sign or symbol. Both types of reflexes are manifestations of groups'
social activity.

Summary

The preoccupation with group cognitive activity in the early days of social psychology did not continue into the present. With the exception of "collective representations," other concepts including "group mind" have not been accepted by the social
psychologists and the study of common beliefs has not been pursued. Neither group
students nor social cognition specialists have been interested in group cognitive
products. Referring to the concept "group mind," G. Allport (1968) stated, "Probably
it is regrettable that the concept was ever used by anyone. We see now that it has
unnecessarily imposed metaphysical blocks in the path of constructive conceptualization" (p. 55). With few exceptions, social psychologists through the years have
studied cognitive processes of individuals and have abandoned their earlier preoccupation with group cognitive activities (Graumann & Moscovici, 1986).

The present contribution focuses on specific mental products of group members,
namely group beliefs (i.e., beliefs that are shared and believed to characterize the
group). In light of the presented review, it is necessary to stress that the present conception of group beliefs suggests that they exist in individuals' minds. The conception
does not suggest that we should view group beliefs as a special superexistential entity
of the group. Beliefs are held by individuals. Organizations, societies, or any other
groups do not hold beliefs on the collective level—only individual members in the
aggregate groups do. However, the present conception describes a widely recognized
phenomenon that group members share beliefs that may come to be viewed as the
defining essence of that group. Sharing indicates neither that group beliefs are supernatural concepts nor that they exist outside of individuals. It merely means that group
members hold the same beliefs due to similar experiences, exposure to common contents, and the influence of social processes. Group beliefs are imparted to new group
members through conventional socialization systems. But group members may at any
time revise the group beliefs by adding, changing, or subtracting beliefs. Members are
not passive carriers of group beliefs, but rather active transmitters who may formulate
and reformulate group beliefs. Group beliefs thus are not stable. Their contents
depend on the specific composition of group members and their experiences.

Chapter 3

The Conception of Group Beliefs

The present conception differentiates among three type of beliefs: *personal beliefs*, *common beliefs*, and *group beliefs*. *Personal beliefs* are those beliefs that individuals perceive as being uniquely their own. These beliefs are not perceived as being shared. Rather, they are believed to be formed by the individuals themselves, and as long as they are not shared, they are considered to be private repertoire. Personal beliefs distinguish individuals from one another by characterizing them as unique persons.

Beliefs that are shared are called *common beliefs*. In these cases, individuals believe that their beliefs are also held by other individuals. Common beliefs can be shared by a small group of family members, friends, members of an organization, members of a society, members of a religion, and even by the majority of human beings. From a specific individual's perspective, common beliefs can be acquired from external sources or formed by himself/herself and later disseminated among other people.

With regard to the former way of acquisition, individuals are aware that their beliefs are shared by other people, since they acquire them from external sources such as other individuals, books, television, radio, or newspapers. Moreover, certain societal institutions, such as mass media or schools, are established in order to provide group members with information that serves as common beliefs. The latter method indicates that individuals create ideas of their own through mental processes labeled as impressions, judgments, inferences, attributions, evaluation, etc., and later share these ideas with other individuals. In turn, the other individuals may adopt these beliefs into their own repertoire of beliefs. In these cases, an individual's personal beliefs disseminate and become common beliefs. All of the shared beliefs, which are not based on experience but on inference, originate from one or several individuals.

One of the most obvious categories of common beliefs is the one that pertains to so-called scientific beliefs that are accepted as facts, such as "The earth revolves around the sun," "Caesar ruled in Rome," "Washington is the capital of the United States," or "Water is a combination of hydrogen and oxygen molecules." Another category refers to experiential beliefs that describe the nature of physical reality, such as "This is a tree," "We sit at a desk," or "It rains." There are no limitations on the subject of common beliefs (see Fletcher, 1984) or the extent of their dissemination.

Of special importance for the present conception are those common beliefs shared by members of the same group. These beliefs are prerequisites for the formation of a social system, and anthropologists advance the idea that a culture may be viewed as a system of common beliefs (e.g., D'Andrade, 1984; Dougherty, 1985). Parsons (1951) argued that "the sharing of common belief system is a condition of the full integration of a system of social interactions" (p. 352). Common beliefs within a group provide the basis that allows group members to maintain their social structure by enabling communication, awareness of similarity, development of interdependence, and coordination of group activity. In this vein, for example, Salisbury (1975) pointed out that what is important in a group, at least from a political point of view, is a display of common attitudes or values. "It is the *shared attitudes* rather than the shared social characteristics which are important" (p. 174) because on their basis group members develop political identity that leads to political action.

The view that groups, through complex interaction between human experiences and intellectual ideas, form belief systems shared by group members has been supported by many social thinkers, including Karl Mannheim, Karl Marx, and Emile Durkheim. These thinkers also realized that the shared beliefs that constitute a group's belief system cannot be reduced to the sum of the properties of personal beliefs. Belief systems in their totality perform important functions in a group's life (e.g., Borhek & Curtis, 1975; Parsons, 1951).

Definition of Group Beliefs

The present conception focuses on a small portion of common beliefs within a group system, which are called *group beliefs*. *Group beliefs are defined as convictions that group members (a) are aware that they share and (b) consider as defining their "groupness."* The first part of the definition suggests that two beliefs have to be shared by group members: One belief pertains to any content that is the subject of group beliefs, and the other belief pertains to the specific content, saying that the former belief is shared by group members. The contents of group beliefs have unlimited scopes. Every content can potentially become a group belief. However, the contents of group beliefs usually pertain to group identity, myths, goals, values, ideology, norms, tradition, or history. The perception of sharing a belief is an important element of the definition. It distinguishes between those beliefs that are considered to be uniquely personal and those beliefs that are viewed to be common. However, it is important to point out that not all common beliefs become group beliefs.

The second part of the definition suggests that group beliefs are those beliefs that define the essence of the group and provide the rationale for the feeling of belonging to the group. Group beliefs provide the cognitive basis that group members view as uniting them into one entity. That is, these beliefs serve as a foundation for group formation and, later, as a bond for group existence. "We are exploited," "Communism is the best system for human beings," "Jesus is God's son," or "Iraq is our enemy" are examples of possible group beliefs.

In fact, group beliefs serve as a raison d'être for a collective of individuals to label themselves as group members and to view the entity as a group. *"We are a group" is the fundamental group belief.* If individuals do not share this belief, then they do not consider themselves to be as group members. Only individuals' awareness that they are group members determines the group's existence for them. (It should be stressed that even when the outside world treats individuals as a group and perceives them as such, the beliefs of these individuals will determine their own reality. If they accept the beliefs of the external world, then their beliefs may change and they may begin to believe that they are a group. But, sometimes, in spite of the common treatment and beliefs of the external world, the individuals may not see themselves as a group). Once the group exists in the individuals' worlds, they can psychologically relate to group characteristics in the form of additional group beliefs. That is, in addition to the fundamental belief "We are a group," group members may share beliefs of various contents pertaining to a variety of other subjects. These beliefs define the uniqueness of the collective of individuals who consider themselves to be a group and serve as anchors for the construction of a coherent system of orientation about the group.

Several examples of group beliefs are provided to illustrate the nature of this concept. In pre-war Japan, and still to a large extent today, part of the Japanese group beliefs concerned the Emperor. The Emperor was believed to be the symbol of the Japanese people, the origin of all morality. Those were shared, unique, beliefs that characterized and, to some extent, still characterize Japanese people. A Japanese document entitled *Cardinal Principles of the National Entity of Japan* explicitly reflects these group beliefs. In the description of identity and solidarity among various symbols and values, it refers to common history ("The great august Will of the Emperor in the administration of the nation is constantly clearly reflected in our history"), to the Emperor ("the Emperor, venerating in person the divine spirits of the Imperial Ancestors, increasingly becomes one in essence with Imperial Ancestry"), and to the value of loyalty ("loyalty means to revere the Emperor as our pivot and to follow him implicitly").

Group beliefs may also be derived from historical events. In this vein, Verba (1965) pointed out that a set of historical events largely determines national identity. The 1917 Bolshevik revolution in Russia and the Mexican revolution in 1910 can be evaluated from this perspective. Both events represent a break with the past and an opening of a new era for the two nations. These two revolutions raised new ideals and goals that the Russians and Mexicans still try to achieve. The beliefs in the significance and positiveness of these events are symbolic; they unify and define the essence of the emerged societies. The beliefs that their revolutions were historical turning points that created new and better societies are group beliefs of both Russians and Mexicans.

Another example of group beliefs can be drawn from the two struggling communities in Northern Ireland. The Protestant community bases its "groupness" on several sets of group beliefs (Roberts, 1971). One set pertains to beliefs regarding the group's "Britishness." The group's loyalty to the Queen and Britain provides group members with special identity in Northern Ireland and differentiates them from the Catholic community. Another set concerns past victories at Derry, Aughrim, and the Boyne, which are linked with the name of William III, Prince of Orange. Finally, the third set of beliefs concerns the religious Protestant content. The Catholic community, on the other hand, maintains group beliefs that refer to its Celtic origin, its willingness to be part of the Irish Republic, and the religious content of Catholicism (Barritt & Carter, 1972).

The Ras Tafari movement, which originated in 1930, in Jamaica, provides an additional example of group beliefs. The basic group beliefs refer to Haile Selassi, the late Emperor of Ethiopia (previously named Ras Tafari), as the living god, view Blacks as true Israelites, and consider the life of the Blacks in British West India as hopeless. In addition, Marcus Garvey, the founder of the movement, who supposedly was sent by Ras Tafari and who disseminated the group beliefs, also spread out the idea that whereas heaven is an invention of the white man, the real heaven is Ethiopia and therefore Blacks should return there (Simpson, 1955).

The principal group beliefs of the John Birch Society, founded in 1958, refer to the opposition to Communism. The beliefs refer to the evilness of this system and declare a war with it.

> We believe that the Communists seek to drive their slaves and themselves along exactly the opposite and downward direction, to the Satanic debasement of both man and his universe. We believe that Communism is as utterly incompatible with all religion as it is contemptuous of all morality and destructive of all freedom. It is "intrinsically evil." It must be opposed, therefore, with equal firmness, on religious grounds, moral grounds, and political grounds. We believe that the continued coexistence of Communism and a Christian-style civilization on one planet is impossible. The struggle between them must end with one completely triumphant and the other completely destroyed. We intend to do our part, therefore, to halt, weaken, rout, and eventually to bury, the whole International Communist Conspiracy. (Welch, 1973, p. 299)

Other group beliefs of the John Birch Society relate to the support of patriotism and a constitutional republic, as well as the rejection of collectivism and the expansion of governmental power (Welch, 1973).

The last two examples illustrate the possible variety of the contents of group beliefs. On the basis of Levy's (1975) detailed analysis of Lubovitcher Hassidim's ethnic identification, it is possible to suggest that the basic group belief of this Jewish religious group is that their Rabbi (Rebbe) personifies all of their core values. This is the Lubovitcher Hassidim's most distinctive group belief, setting the group apart from other Hassidic groups. Also, Thompson and Peterson's (1975) description indicates that the basic group belief of the Choctaw Indians in Mississippi refers to speaking the Choctaw language. As the tribal chairman said, "If he speaks Choctaw, he's Choctaw."

Group Beliefs and Group Definitions

The proposed conception has special importance for group definition. It implies that group beliefs are essential elements of the definition of any type of group, as long as the self-perception of individuals as group members is considered a necessary condition for group existence. In the framework of this condition (i.e., the "subjective" perspective), in order to consider their entity to be a group, group members have to believe that they constitute a group and/or that they have something in common that unites them (though additional conditions are also possible). Thus, while some definitions that include this condition refer only to the fundamental group belief "We are a group," others include various group beliefs such as goals, ideologies, values, common attributes, or identities. The coming review not only points out the different contents of group beliefs, but also indicates that they are used in definitions of different types of groups.

Among the definitions of the subjective perspective, we find those of Deutsch (1968), who stated that "a psychological group exists (has unity) to the extent that the individuals composing it perceive themselves as pursuing promotively interdependent goals" (p. 468), and of Smith (1945), who defined a group as "a unit consisting of a plural number of separate organism (agents) who have a collective perception of their unity and who have the ability to act and/or are acting in a unitary manner toward their environment" (p. 227). Thus, according to Deutsch, group members have to hold a group belief regarding an interdependent goal, while, according to Smith, they have to hold a belief about being a group.

Similarly, Olmsted (1959) defined a group "as a plurality of individuals who are in contact with one another, who take one another into account, and who are aware of some significant commonality" (p. 21). He points out that "an example feature of a group is that its members have something in common and that they believe that what they have in common makes a difference" (pp. 21–22). In other words, group members have to hold group beliefs in order to be a group. Tajfel and Turner (1979) also take the subjective perspective and define a group

> as a collection of individuals who perceive themselves to be members of the same social category, share some emotional involvement in this common definition of themselves, and achieve some degree of social consensus about the evaluation of their group and their membership of it. (p. 40)

In a similar way, Merton (1957) includes the subjective criterion in his definition. He proposed that

> the sociological concept of a group refers to a number of people who interact with one another in accord with established patterns.... A second criterion of a group ... is that the interacting persons define themselves as "members", i.e. that they have patterned expectations of forms of interaction which are morally binding on them and on other members, but not on those regarded as "outside" the group. The correlative and third criterion is that the person in interaction be defined by others as "belonging to the group," these others including fellow-members and non-members. (pp. 285–286)

Finally, in their classic book *Group Dynamics*, Cartwright and Zander (1968) provided a list of group characteristics that are included in the various definitions proposed by different theorists. The list indicates that five out of ten characteristics may be seen as referring to group beliefs as follows: ". . . (b) they define themselves as members," ". . . (d) they share norms concerning matters of common interest," ". . . (f) they identify with one another as a result of having set up the same model-object or ideals in their super-ego," ". . . (h) they pursue promotively interdependent goals," and "(i) they have a collective perception of their unity" (p. 48).

The subjective perspective used to define a group is not limited to a definition of small groups, but can also be used to define macro groups such as social movements, ethnic groups, societies, or nations.

Thus, Krech and Crutchfield (1948), who differentiated between social groups (informal entities of relatively small size and short duration) and social organizations, defined the latter concept as "specific groupings of actual people, which are characterized by the possession of the following: (1) cultural products (such as buildings, robes, prayers, magic, formulas, songs); (2) a collective name or symbol; (3) distinctive action patterns; (4) a common belief system; and (5) enforcing agents or techniques" (p. 369). Similarly, Killian (1964) suggested four characteristics to define a large group constituting a social movement. Three of them referred to shared beliefs:

> 1. The existence of shared values — a goal or an objective, sustained by an ideology.
> 2. A sense of membership or participation — a "we-ness", a distinction between those who are for and those against. 3. Norms — shared understandings as to how the followers should act, definitions of outgroups and how to behave toward them. (p. 431)

Shared beliefs were also proposed to define ethnic groups (e.g., Barth, 1969a; De Vos, 1975). De Vos's definition suggests viewing an ethnic group as a

> self-perceived group of people who hold in common a set of traditions shared by the others with whom they are in contact. Such tradition typically includes "folk" religious beliefs and practices, language, a sense of historical continuity, and common ancestry or place of origin. (p. 9)

In the present framework, it is not surprising that many anthropologists insist on the necessity of the "emic" approach in the study of the identity question. This approach concentrates on the beliefs of the groups. In the case of the ethnic research, it tries to identify the subjective symbolic use of any aspect of culture that ethnic groups utilize to differentiate themselves from other groups (e.g., Barth, 1969b).

Finally, Aberle, Cohen, Davis, Levy, and Sutton (1950), who defined functional conditions for a society, include two provisions that directly refer to group beliefs: "The members must share a body of cognitive orientations" and "they must share certain goals, that have common modes of feeling and willing" (p. 101). Similarly, Emerson (1960) proposed that "the simplest statement that can be made about a nation is that it is a body of people who feel that they are a nation; and it may be that when all the time-spun analysis is concluded this will be the ultimate statement as well" (p. 102).

It should be noted that not all of the definitions of a group take a subjective perspective. Some definitions provide a so-called "external" or "objective" criterion for group existence, ignoring shared beliefs of group members. In this category there are definitions that focus on such organizational characteristics of a group as properties of statuses, roles, and interactions. For example, Stogdill (1959) defined a group as "an open interaction system in which actions determine the structure of the system and successive interactions exert coequal effects upon the identity of the system" (p. 18), and Shaw (1976) defined a group "as two or more persons who are interacting with one another in such a manner that each person influences, and is influenced by each other person" (p. 11).

The present conception refers to a group as a general concept. *The proposed definition states that a group is a collective of individuals with a defined sense of membership and shared beliefs, including group beliefs; which regulate their behavior at least in matters related to the collective.* This definition encompasses groups of various sizes and kinds including small groups, associations, organizations, political parties, interest groups, religious denominations, ethnic groups, and even nations. *The three necessary and sufficient conditions for a collective to be a group are: (a) Individuals in the collective should define themselves as group members; (b) they should share beliefs, including group beliefs; and (c) there should be some level of coordinated activity.*

It must be realized that the concept *group*, as used throughout the book, is very general and encompasses many types of groups. In order to deal with this variety, social scientists have suggested various categories to classify groups. Cartwright and Zander (1968) pointed out in this vein that

> a common procedure has been to select a few properties and to define "types" of groups on the basis of whether these properties are present or absent. Among the properties most often employed are: size (number of members), amount of physical interaction among members, degree of intimacy, level of solidarity, locus of control of group activities, extent of formalization of rules governing relations among members and tendency of members to react to one another as individual persons or as occupants of roles. Although it would be possible to construct a large number of types of groups by combining these properties, in various ways, usually only dichotomies have resulted: formal-informal, primary-secondary, small-large, Gemeinschaft-Gesellschaft, autonomous-dependent, temporary-permanent, consensual-symbiotic. Sometimes a rather different procedure has been advocated in which groups are classified according to their objectives or social settings. (p. 24)

Obviously this comprehensive statement does not exhaust all the possible criteria for group categorization. Nevertheless, from the present perspective all groups have to have members who perceive themselves as being part of this entity and all of them have to have group beliefs as partial necessary conditions.

How central the group beliefs are to the members, how much confidence group members have in them, or how functional they are to the individuals and the group are questions that are related to various group properties. It is suggested that the centrality, confidence, and functionality of group beliefs are not necessarily related to the size of the group. Large groups such as nations, ethnic groups, or religious denominations, as well as small groups such as professional organizations, sects, or interest groups have group beliefs, which may vary in these characteristics. *One significant variable that determines the status of group beliefs is the importance of the group for group members. Groups are important and group beliefs become central in group members' repertoire when they satisfy group members' needs.* Group beliefs of small groups as well as large ones can fulfill this function.

The study of group beliefs should not be restricted to specific groups, but should encompass all types of groups. Their examination not only sheds special light on the essence of the group phenomenon itself, but also on various group processes and structures.

With the above point, it should be emphasized that the present view *does not suggest viewing a mere self-categorization of individuals as a sufficient condition for group existence.* It differentiates between individuals who classify themselves as a category and group members who, in addition to self-classification as group members, are also interdependent in their behavior (Horwitz & Rabbie, 1989; Rabbie & Horwitz, 1988). Although it is recognized that a necessary first step in group formation is self-categorization (which will be discussed later), another necessary condition involves at least some level of coordinated activity, which does not have to involve face-to-face interaction. According to Rabbie and Horwitz (1988), the movement from the initial step of self-categorization takes place "when the group is viewed as a locomoting entity, one that actively moves or passively moves in its environment toward or away from group harm or benefit" (p. 119).

This conception goes beyond the "mere categorization" condition for group existence as suggested by Tajfel (1981) and Turner (1987). It does recognize the importance of the fundamental group belief, "We are a group," for group formation. But, at the same time, it suggests that in order for a category of individuals to become a group, there is a need to form additional group beliefs that define the nature of the "groupness" and to develop a coordinated activity that reflects interdependence. The latter condition is based on Lewin's (1951) conception of a group, which proposed that a group as a dynamic whole depends on "the interdependence of the members (or better, of the subparts of the group)" (p. 146).

In conclusion, leaving aside for the didactic purpose the condition of coordinated activity, the subjective approach to a group suggests that until individuals begin to believe that they are a group, they are not—at least in accordance to their own reality. Thus, individuals may be perceived as acting as a group and be labeled as such by various individuals and groups, but as long as they do not perceive themselves as a group, they are not, in their eyes. A group exists for these individuals only if it exists in their phenomenological field. This approach focuses, as will be described later, on a sequence of processes leading from experiences through perception to self-categorization as a group.

Accordingly, there might be disagreement between beliefs. A collective of individuals may consider themselves as a group, while observers may disagree with this perception. Conversely, observers may consider a collective of individuals to be a group, while the individuals perceived to be a group may not think so. The question can thus be raised: In which perspective is one interested? Since, according to the philosophical foundation presented in the first chapter, beliefs are relative and subjective, the answer depends on the object of the inquiry. If one is interested in studying the phenomenology of the individuals constituting the collective, then one should focus the inquiry on their beliefs. This approach has many theoretical bases, but one assumption related to this direction of inquiry has special importance for understanding group behavior: namely, that individuals act consistently with their beliefs (e.g., Brunswick, 1956; Heider, 1958; Krech & Crutchfield, 1948). Thus, individuals' perception of whether they are a group or not determines to a large extent their behavior.

An interesting point was raised by Tajfel (1981) with regard to "objective" and "subjective" definitions. He noted that the "outside objective and uncommitted" observers and group members may use similar "tools" to establish group characteristics and boundaries. "But"—as Tajfel rightly suggested—

> the criteria for accepting the validity of one construction or another may differ vastly between those who engage in the "outside" construction for their professional (scientific) purposes and those inside the system who need guidelines for their behavior and thus attempt to construct a coherent system of orientation in their social environment. (p. 46)

The belief "We are a group" is part of the reality of the individuals who constitute a group. For them, the group is real. They talk, feel, behave, and form other beliefs in the framework of the group that exists for them. They use the terms "we," "our group," "other groups." They see the forest (the Gestalt) and not only the trees. Therefore, group members refer to common activities, goals, past, interdependence, etc., and act accordingly. The most important implication derived from the subjective definition for the present analysis is that groups do have group beliefs that constitute their essential characteristics. In other words, as indicated earlier, the subjective approach indicates that a collective of individuals has to have at least one group belief stating "We are a group" as a first step to consider itself as a group. Nevertheless, groups usually have more than one group belief. Groups may have numerous group beliefs pertaining to many different contents.

The existence of beliefs shared by group members, who are aware of this fact, and the implications of this phenomenon for the lives of group members stress the necessity to focus on the study of these beliefs. Such direction of interest should include all the themes that have fascinated social psychologists in their investigation of personal beliefs—that is, the acquisition, characteristics, function, structure, influence on individual and group behavior, and antecedents of group beliefs. All of these topics are subjects of this book.

Identification of Group Beliefs

Group beliefs, as implied by the definition, are held by group members. They share these beliefs and consider them as characterizing their group. Therefore, group members should be the subjects of an inquiry into group beliefs. They can report shared beliefs that characterize them as a group. The study of group beliefs through group members is the direct way to identify these beliefs. This direction of research can be based on interviews or questionnaires of group members or their samples.

A study by Deconchy (1984) provides a good example of how group beliefs may be investigated, although the investigator had different objectives and did not report the results, which are of interest for the present purpose. The study concerned group beliefs of the Catholic Church and was carried out among representatives of the Catholic Church system (priests, teachers of catechism, monks, nuns, and seminarians). The participants in the study were presented with 18 propositions, which either expressed classic shared beliefs of the group or contradicted them in an ambiguous way. The respondents were asked to sort the propositions into the following four categories: (1) "I believe it, and all those who wish to be members of my Church must also believe it"; (2) "I believe it, but someone who does not could still be a member of my Church"; (3) "I do not believe it, but someone who does could still be a member of my Church"; and (4) "I do not believe it and someone who does could not be, in any circumstances, a member of my Church." The described method of this study pertains to the basic function of group beliefs — demarcation of group boundaries.

The question of measuring shared beliefs in a group is not unique to the specific problem of assessing group beliefs. Political scientists, sociologists, and psychologists have tried to measure categories of shared beliefs that may be considered as group beliefs. For example, Szalay and Kelly (1982) provided an example using the Associative Group Analysis (see Szalay & Deese, 1978) to measure ideology among different groups. The method is constructed to elicit free verbal association in order to assess the content of the responses and their frequencies of appearance. In their first study, Szalay and Kelly (1982) reported the meaning of the concepts capitalism, communism, socialism, and Marxism to a sample of Slovenians in Yugoslavia and to a sample of Americans. The second study focused on the meaning of the concepts of democracy and politics to Koreans and Americans.

Another attempt to assess shared belief was done by Jackson (1965). He developed a method to measure the extent of approval or disapproval of a norm by group members. His method allows the establishment of the degree of consensus and the intensity of support or disagreement. A number of reported studies show that Jackson and his students were able to measure the characteristics of norms within small groups and organizations.

One important problem in measuring group beliefs is that group members may disagree in their reports on which beliefs are included in such a set. Nevertheless, it is assumed that although group members may not achieve consensus in describing all of the beliefs, they should be able to point to the most important group beliefs (i.e., of high centrality) with considerable consensus. In fact, the level of agreement may serve as one indicator of group belief importance. The degree of consensus that is reported correlates to the degree of indication that the group belief is basic. Some beliefs may be more prototypic to group characterization than others.

The extent to which members of a group agree on group beliefs or other shared information within a group has been of interest for social scientists. For example, anthropologists Romney, Weller, and Batchelder (1986) developed a formal mathematical model for the analysis of culture knowledge based on the consensus among group members. The model is based on patterns of agreements among group members that allow them to make inferences about their differential knowledge of shared beliefs. Although the model was tested on few respondents, according to the researchers, it opens the possibility of measuring the "cultural competence of informants in a variety of domains" (p. 323). Within the present framework, it may be used to assess shared knowledge of group beliefs.

Although group beliefs are part of individuals' cognitive repertoires, they also may be manifested in various group products. The manifestation can be either implicit or explicit. In the first case, group beliefs may be inferred from various verbal outputs such as leaders' speeches, documents, or books. Content analysis of these outputs may reveal group beliefs. One example of this research direction is Coleman's (1941) attempt to define the specific characteristics of Americans. He based his study on content analysis of a random sample of books and periodicals written by contemporary and earlier authors. The units of analysis were statements that distinctively characterize all the Americans. The final list of American traits on which most authors agreed consisted of 27 items. Among them were such characteristics as a belief in democracy, a belief in individualism, a belief in the importance of education, a belief in equality, and a belief that it is a duty and a virtue to make money. Although the study did not investigate American group beliefs per se, it does suggest a way of approaching their examination.

The explicit way of manifesting group beliefs indicates that they are formally presented in group products, such as in documents and books. A group may publicize what is considered to be group beliefs. Many groups publicize their goals, ideology, history, and so on, which are formally presented as their group beliefs.

In this regard, it should be noted that there may be a lack of correspondence between group members' reports on what constitutes group beliefs and formal presentations of group beliefs. A lack of correspondence may be caused by at least one or more of the following: (a) The formalized presentation of group beliefs was not updated in view of group belief changes; (b) the presentation indicates possible future changes in group beliefs, as desired by the leadership; (c) the presentation represents a minority opinion that is not part of the consensus; (d) the presentation describes a set of beliefs on which there is a disagreement within a group; or (e) the presentation describes the ideal desired beliefs. Some of these phenomena will be analyzed in later chapters. Although the definition in this chapter focused on group members' beliefs, the formalized presentation of group beliefs cannot be underestimated. Since the formalized presentation often serves as a symbolic representation of the group, the group pays special attention to its content. Many of a group's social processes concern formulation and reformulation of these statements. Moreover, these formulations, as representations of group beliefs, are the foci around which group change takes place. Mergers or splits in a group, as will be discussed later, are based on agreements and disagreements with the formalized group beliefs.

This book relies mostly on formal formulations of group beliefs in written materials, or their analysis by observers (i.e., social scientists) in the examples provided, since there is very little available research on group members' reports. These examples should be viewed as illustrations of the proposed conception.

Summary

This chapter introduces the concept of group beliefs as a framework for analyzing groups. Group members share group beliefs, are aware of this sharing, and believe that group beliefs define their "groupness." The contents of group beliefs provide the raison d'être for a group's existence and delineate its uniqueness vis-à-vis other groups. The fundamental group belief indicates that the group exists. In addition, group members may add other group beliefs of a wide scope of contents covering such themes as the group's common history, ideology, or goals.

Although human beings are members of very different groups, all of them have group beliefs if they believe that they constitute a group. Since the self-categorization of individuals as group members is considered a necessary condition for group existence, group beliefs, as characteristics of a collective, are important elements of a group's definition.

In spite of the fact that identifying group beliefs in certain groups is easier than in others, group beliefs play an important role in every group's life. Group members themselves should report their group beliefs. But, since it is not possible in every group to collect these reports, other means of inquiry into group beliefs are suggested. One way of detecting group beliefs is to examine group products, either as inferences from verbal outputs from various sources such as leaders, or as formally written presentations in written materials. The next chapter will provide numerous examples of formally presented beliefs that may be considered as explicit manifestations of group beliefs.

Chapter 4

Contents and Characteristics of Group Beliefs

After the presentation of the conception, this chapter further describes the nature of group beliefs by providing more examples of possible contents and discussing their characteristics.

Contents of Group Beliefs

As indicated in Chapter 3, group beliefs may consist of any contents, which can be of unlimited scopes. This is one of the basic premises of the present conception. It is assumed that every self-defined group has group beliefs as a definition for its "we-ness." Since groups are of different types, are established in order to achieve different goals, have different histories, act in different environments, and are made up of different members and structures, the contents of group beliefs vary. They may refer to religious doctrines, political ideologies, philanthropic goals, human rights issues, identity characteristics, and many other subjects.

   The following examples provide illustrations of the diversity of contents. The American Sunbathing Society published the following principles, which can be considered as its group beliefs:

> We *believe* in the essential wholesomeness of the human body, and all its functions.
> We *endeavor* to foster the desire to improve and perfect the body by natural living in the out-of-doors.
> We *believe* the sunshine and fresh air in immediate contact with the entire body are basic factors in maintaining healthy bodies.
> We *believe* presentation of the male and female figures in their entirety and completeness needs no apology or defense and that only in such an attitude of mind can we find true modesty.
> We *accord* to every part of the body an equally normal naturalness wholly devoid of any vulgarity or obscenity. In this view an elbow, a pubic arch, or a nose, are equally respectable.
> We *believe* that children raised in the nudist philosophy will be healthier in mind and body. They will learn to look on life as being essentially pure. *Nudism* will teach

them moral and physical cleanliness; never to degrade but keep their thoughts and actions clean.
Our Goal? A healthy mind in a healthy body.
(Toch, 1965, pp. 21–22, copied from *Information About Nudism and the A.S.A.*, Mays Landing, NJ: The American Sunbathing Association, undated)

The group beliefs of Amalgamated Flying Saucer Clubs of America are stated in the following way:

We affirm that flying saucers are real, that in reality they are true spacecraft manned by people from other planets, who are visiting and making contact with various persons of our planet for the purpose of imparting information which can be used for the benefit of all men of earth. We deplore the actions of our government in withholding information on this subject which is so vital to the welfare of our nation and its people.
(Toch, 1965, p. 24, copied from *AFSCA World Report*, Amalgamated Flying Saucer Clubs of America, July–August, 1960)

It can be assumed that group members of each of these groups confidently hold their group beliefs, which provide identity and characterize their uniqueness.

As was proposed, the fundamental group belief refers to the perceived reality of the group members, indicating that they are a group. "We are a group" is a necessary belief for group existence that frames both the personal and group identity. Tajfel (1981) suggested that this belief may include from one to three components:

A cognitive component, in the sense of the knowledge that one belongs to a group; an evaluative one, in the sense that the notion of the group and/or of one's member-ship in it may have a positive or a negative value connotation; and an emotional component in the sense that the cognitive and evaluative aspects of the group and one's membership in it may be accompanied by emotions (such as love or hatred, like or dislike) directed towards one's own group and towards others which stand in certain relations to it. (p. 229)

On the basis of the fundamental group belief, other group beliefs are added. Their contents may pertain to the totality of group members' lives or refer to a very specific subject that characterizes the particular group. In the first case, the group beliefs may cover contents of all the aspects of group members' lives by referring to a wide range of norms, values, goals, means, and so on. In these groups, members are required to live a certain life-style as dictated by group beliefs. This is the case, for example, with certain religious groups (e.g., Amish society or Orthodox Jews) or with certain ideological groups (e.g., revolutionary groups). In the other case, group beliefs refer to a narrow aspect of group members' lives and pertain to a specific content. For example, the content may relate to a particular goal such as protecting the natural environment (e.g, Sierra Club) or protecting an unborn child's right to live (e.g,. National Right to Life Committee). Nevertheless, the classifica-tion is not dichotomous, but represents a continuum of which the two extreme poles have been described. Groups differ with regard to the extent to which their group beliefs cover various aspects of group members' lives.

Group beliefs can be divided into different categories. The categories can be based on various criteria and used for different purposes. In this chapter, as examples of the wide scope of the possible contents of group beliefs, the following four categories, which are widely used by behavioral scientists, will be discussed: norms, values, goals, and ideology. The purpose of this discussion is to show that the concept of group beliefs does not overlap with previously used categories, but provides a unique perspective for these specific group characteristics. That is, the conception suggests that these categories may not necessarily serve as group beliefs. Thus, definitions of each category and their implications for the group beliefs' conception will be presented, including examples of group beliefs in each category.[1]

Group Norms

Group norms are shared standards that guide group members' behavior (Smelser, 1967). Based on cultural values, tradition, and goals (McCall & Simmons, 1982), norms tell group members what they should or should not do, prescribing appropriate behavior and indicating inappropriate ones. As Homans (1950) stated, a norm is "an idea in the minds of the members of a group, an idea that can be put in the form of a statement specifying what the members or other men should do, ought to do, are expected to do, under given circumstances" (p. 123). Thus, norms regulate group members' behavior and provide criteria for judging it.

Norms, as defined, do not necessarily have to be group beliefs. Norms may regulate group members' behavior without being considered as characteristic of the specific group. In such groups, group beliefs pertain to contents other than norms. In other groups, at least part of the norms may define their characteristics and be group beliefs. Even in these instances, however, not all of the norms may be of equal importance in defining a group's uniqueness. Nevertheless, when norms function as group beliefs, group members believe that their patterns of behavior are unique to them and characterize their membership. Adherence to certain types of food, clothing, observance of rituals, and kinds of interactions differentiates group members and out-groups.

In an extensive description of Amish society, Hostetler (1968) points out several norms that can be considered as group beliefs. For example, Amish preaching prescribes the necessity of separation from the world. Therefore, an Amish man does not marry a non-Amish woman, does not do business with an outsider, and even does not enter into intimate relationships with a person outside the Amish community. In addition to norms of separation, the Amish group also perpetuates norms of

---

[1]Most of the examples provided in the following review are drawn from formal statements prepared by the groups. Although it is possible that they reflect the group beliefs, group members were not examined to indicate their responses. Therefore, the presented "group beliefs" should be treated with caution. They only serve as illustrations for presenting the conception. Further research among group members may determine the actual status of these beliefs.

nonresistance. Group members are forbidden to take part in violence or war, and they withdraw from conflicts or resistance. They refuse to swear any oath, to bear arms, or to hold public offices.

Through the ceremony of baptism, adolescents become full members in the church. From that time, they and other group members are committed to maintaining the rules of the church (Ordnung). The rules are not specified in writing, but they are known to every group member. They cover the whole range of human experience. They forbid the use of electricity, telephones, automobiles, or tractors; they require hooks-and-eyes on dresscoats and the use of horses for farming and travel. No formal education beyond the elementary grades is a rule of life. The following passage specifies some of the rules:

> No ornamental bright, showy form-fitting, immodest or silk-like clothing of any kind. Colors such as bright red, orange, yellow and pink not allowed. Amish form of clothing to be followed as a general rule. Costly Sunday clothing to be discouraged. Dresses not shorter than half-way between knees and floor, nor over eight inches from floor. Longer advisable. Clothing in every way modest, serviceable and as simple as scripturally possible. Only outside pockets allowed are one on work eberhem or vomas and pockets on large overcoats. Dress shoes, if any, to be plain and black only. No high heels and pomp slippers, dress socks, if any, to be black except white for foot hygiene for both sexes. A plain, unshowy suspender without buckles.
>
> Hat to be black with no less than 3-inch rim and not extremely high in crown. No stylish impression in any hat. No pressed trousers. No sweaters.
>
> Prayer covering to be simple, and made to fit head. Should cover all the hair as nearly as possible and is to be worn wherever possible. [Pleating of caps to be discouraged.] No silk ribbons. Young children to dress according to the Word as well as parents. No pink or fancy baby blankets or caps.
>
> Women to wear shawls, bonnets, and capes in public. Aprons to be worn at all times. No adorning of hair among either sex such as parting of hair among men and curling or waving among women.
>
> A full beard should be worn among men and boys after baptism if possible. No shingled hair. Length at least half-way below tops of ears.
>
> No decorations of any kind in buildings inside or out. No fancy yard fences. Linoleum, oilcloth, shelf and wall paper to be plain and unshowy. Over-stuffed furniture or any luxury items forbidden. No doilies or napkins. No large mirrors, (fancy glassware), statues or wall pictures for decorations. (Hostetler, 1968, pp. 59–60)

In another example, Ardener (1983) described the group beliefs of Canadian Doukhobors who emigrated from Russia at the beginning of the twentieth century. They believe that the Perfect Life is attainable on earth through the rejection of materialism. They have not recognized human authority structure and therefore are opposed to state legislation or oath taking. Their uniqueness has been reflected in deprivation, suffering, and poverty, which became, according to Ardener, part of their self-definition, corresponding to their identification with Christ himself. In this vein, to form their own identity, Doukhobors resorted to nudity as a social artifact for identifying their group and to the use of arson against institutions and then against their own property. Ardener suggested that both practices helped to maintain the boundary of the group and to enhance solidarity in the face of outgroups.

Group Values

An analysis similar to the one presented about norms applies to group values. Groups may hold values, but they do not necessarily have to function as group beliefs. A value is defined as "an enduring belief that a specific mode of conduct or end-state of existence is . . . socially preferable to an opposite or converse mode of conduct or end-state of existence" (Rokeach, 1973, p. 5). The former is called an instrumental value, while the latter is called a terminal value.

Unlike norms, values do not specify particular patterns of behaviors, but they do provide abstract ideas and long-range concerns, which guide the selection of the means and ends of specific actions, and serve as criteria by which objects, actions, or events are evaluated. Thus, individuals may have many norms or attitudes and few values. Examples of values are freedom, truth, individualism, or equality. They reflect the ideals to which individuals and groups aspire.

Individuals differ with regard to the values they hold or consider as important. However, beyond the individual differences, it is possible to characterize groups by the values that their group members share (Kluckhohn, 1951; Parsons, 1968). Sociologists have focused on shared values, referring to them as value systems in a given society. Nevertheless, a given shared value is not necessarily held by every person in the group. When a sufficient number of group members subscribe to the value, it may not only characterize the group, but may also become an important determinant of the group members' behavior.

Williams (1960) suggested some concrete tests of value dominance within a group. Specifically, he stated that within a group, the dominance of values can be evaluated according to the following four criteria: (a) extensiveness of the value in the total activity of the system, measured in terms of the proportion of the population and of its activities that manifest the value; (b) duration of the value, measured in terms of the persistence of the value over a period of time; (c) intensity with which the value is sought or maintained, measured in terms of effort, crucial choices, verbal affirmation, and reactions to threats to the value; and (d) prestige of value carriers; that is, of persons, objects, or organizations considered to be bearers of the value (measured in terms of heroes, high status, reputation, etc.). (These criteria can be also used for evaluating group beliefs.)

In some groups the values, like norms, may be formally formulated (i.e., in writing) and maintained as group beliefs, while in other groups, they are never formally defined, but may be considered as group beliefs and carried latently through the social processes of socialization and influence. However, in both types of groups, when values are shared by group members and viewed by them as characterizing the group, they are group beliefs. In this case, the value or values define the uniqueness of the group and differentiate it from out-groups.

To specify values that characterize a nation is a complex task. Nevertheless, social scientists commonly have suggested, on the basis of either collected data or their own observations, that self-sufficient individualism is one of the salient characteristics of American society (e.g., Diamond, 1976; Gillin, 1955; Slater, 1970; Williams, 1960, 1970). This value emphasizes the responsibility and the right of each individual to pursue personal goals in as much freedom from restraints as possible. Americans are socialized to internalize this value and to believe that it characterizes their society.

Many groups present values as part of their credo. In fact, many of the group norms and goals functioning as group beliefs are based on values. This stress on values can be observed in religious groups, as well as in many political groups. For example, Whitworth (1971) described the emergence of a Utopian sect formally known as "The Society of Brothers" or as "the Bruderhof." The sect was established in Germany during the 1920s by Eberhard Arnold. The group beliefs referred to values and norms of early true Christians as models for a new society. Specifically, Arnold preached the values of charity, equality, nonviolence, and simplicity, which were reflected in the group members' sharing of all possessions and labor, refusing to vote and hold office, refusing to serve in the army, wearing simple clothing, and so on. These beliefs made the sect unique and differentiated it from out-groups.

An example of a political group that was founded on the basis of a value is Amnesty International. In its statute, the value of human rights underlies more specific goals. The beginning reads:

1. Considering that every person has the right freely to hold and to express his or her convictions and the obligation to extend a like freedom to others, the objects of Amnesty International shall be to secure throughout the world the observance of the provisions of the Universal Declaration of Human Rights, by:
   a) irrespective of political considerations working towards the release of and providing assistance to persons who in violation of the aforesaid provisions are imprisoned, detained or otherwise physically restricted by reason of their political, religious or other conscientiously held beliefs or by reason of their ethnic origin, sex, color, or language, provided that they had not used or advocated violence (hereinafter referred to as "Prisoners of Conscience");
   b) opposing by all appropriate means the detention of any Prisoners of Conscience or any political prisoners without trial within a reasonable time or any trial procedures relating to such prisoners that do not conform to internationally recognized norms;
   c) opposing by all appropriate means the imposition and infliction of death penalties and torture or other cruel, inhuman or degrading treatment or punishment of prisoners or other detained or restricted persons whether or not they have used or advocated violence.

                                    (Amnesty International pamphlet, London, 1978)

Although the Ku Klux Klan is vastly different from Amnesty International, its group beliefs are also based on values. The principal beliefs of the Ku Klux Klan are presented in the following way:

> We invite all men who can qualify to become citizens of the Invisible Empire, to approach the portal of our beneficent domain, join us in our noble work of extending its boundaries, and in disseminating the gospel of Klankraft, thereby encouraging, conserving, protecting and making vital the fraternal relationship in the practice of an honorable clannishness; to share with us the sacred duty of protecting womanhood; to maintain forever the God-given supremacy of the White Race; to commemorate the holy and chivalric achievement of our fathers, to safeguard the sacred rights, privileges and institutions of our civil government; to bless mankind and to keep eternally ablaze the sacred fire of a fervent devotion to a pure Americanism. (Vander Zanden, 1960, p. 290)

Thus, the values of womanhood, white supremacy, mankind, and Americanism are the values that the group intends to protect.

Group Goals

Group goals are defined as beliefs of valued or desired future specific states for the group (Cartwright & Zander, 1968; Etzioni, 1975a). On the basis of this definition, we can assume that with few exceptions almost all groups have goals. Some groups, for example, may focus on mere function of having social relationship or on routine functions to maintain status quo (Korten, 1962). Despite such exceptions, instrumental and well-defined goals play a significant role in the life of many groups. In most of these cases, goals may serve as group beliefs in addition to other beliefs. Individuals form groups to achieve certain goals. Subsequently, goals are often considered as a raison d'être for group formation, frequently keep group members together, provide a basis for solidarity, and give direction for activity. These functions are particularly explicit in certain voluntary groups that are formed to advance specific goals (Sills, 1958). Thus, it is not surprising that group goals frequently serve as basic group beliefs. They increase the identification of the group members with their group and define the boundary for group membership. In this vein, March and Simon (1958) noted that:

> The greater the extent to which goals are perceived as shared among members of a group, the stronger the propensity of the individual to identify with the group and vice versa. (p. 66)

Several examples of group goals may provide illustrations of how they function as group beliefs. Trans-Species Unlimited (TSU) is a national animal rights group "dedicated to the total elimination of animal abuse and exploitation." This group belief leads the TSU to direct actions and legislative campaigns to end such practices as the use of the leghold trap and live bird shoots and commercial exploitation of rabbits for meat, fur, and research.

The International Kolping Society, founded in the middle of the previous century in Germany by Adolph Kolping, aims today:

> to enable its members, as Christians of the world, to give a good account of themselves in their occupations, marriages, families, the church, society as a whole, and the state, to serve the needs of its members and society as a whole, to promote

general welfare in the Christian spirit through active participation of its members, individually or as a group, and to take part in the continuing improvement of
society.
(copied from the pamphlet *International Kolping Society: Founder, Aims, Tasks*,
Cologne, 1979)

On the basis of these group beliefs the society engages in various community activities to help individuals and the group. The Richard III Society was founded in
England in 1924 to:

1. To promote in every possible way historical research into the life and times of
   King Richard III.
2. To secure a reassessment of the historical material relating to this period and of
   the role in English history of this monarch.
3. To circulate all relevant historical information to members of the Society and to
   educational authorities.
   (copied from the pamphlet of The Richard III Society, New Orleans, undated)

The principal goal of this group is to present the truthful history of King Richard III
in view of past distortions and biases.

Groups differ with regard to the goals that they try to achieve. There is a variety
of goals that can be classified into different categories. One type of category has
received special attention by political scientists—namely, goals to influence governmental decisions. Groups that have these goals are called *interest groups* (Salisbury,
1975), and the term *interest* denotes a "shared attitude toward what is needed or
wanted in a given situation, observable as demands, or claims upon other groups in
the society" (Truman, 1951, p. 33). These shared demands or claims, which reflect
goals, serve as a basis for group formation and therefore function as group beliefs.
The interests can pertain to various contents involving either tangible or intangible
claims, and concerns of either a particular policy objective or wide societal goals
(Salisbury, 1975).

Interest groups can be based on either a few or many group beliefs. Interest
groups, such as some liberal and conservative groups in the United States, may
adopt far-reaching political beliefs covering a wide spectrum of policy areas. Americans for Democratic Action (ADA) and The Conservative Caucus (TCC) are examples, respectively, of durable and important liberal and conservative ideological
interest groups. TCC lists 10 principles (some are values) that may be considered as
group beliefs:

1. Right to Enjoy the Income From One's Own Labor
   There should be a ceiling on the proportion of income which government may take
   away, in taxes, from any citizen. Graduated taxation, combined with inflation,
   places an especially unfair burden on working Americans, whose tax rates increase
   automatically, as inflation pushes them into higher tax brackets.
2. Right to Personal Security
   Citizens have the right to the security of their persons, their homes, and their
   property. It is the first task of government to protect the law-abiding from those who
   break the law. Concern for the rights of crime's victims must be emphasized over
   the privileges of those who commit crimes. The goal of law enforcement should be
   to apprehend, punish, and isolate those who criminally violate the rights of others.

3. Right to Educational Freedom
   The right of parents to define the conditions and content of their children's education must outweigh the power of government to interfere in the selection of textbooks or teachers, or to use the schools to advance the political, cultural and social objectives of government officials. There must be no forced busing.
4. Right to Religious Liberty
   The government should not be permitted to interfere with the freedom of individuals to pray to God in accordance with their own beliefs; nor should there be any officially established orthodoxy, religious or secular.
5. Right to Life
   No government resources should be used to encourage, sanction, or assist in the taking of innocent human life.
6. Right to National Sovereignty
   The defense policy of the United States should be based on a goal of strategic and tactical supremacy on land, in the sea, in the air, and in space. Our foreign policy should have as its sole and overriding purpose safeguarding the national interest.
7. Right to Economic Justice
   The government should be required to hold the level of its income and not print or coin new money to meet governmental obligations, thus inflating the currency and deflating the value of money already in circulation. The principal victims of government over-spending are the working men and women of America whose income is reduced in value and whose jobs are threatened by the inflation and unemployment which results from a public sector grown too large.
8. Right to Be Individually Judged
   Quotas, based on characteristics inherited at birth, are both discriminatory and arbitrary, wrongfully disregarding individual merit, achievement, and successful competition in favor of collective classifications. The government should not apply or encourage the use of quotas as a basis of selection in education, employment, or conferring of benefits. Individual rights must, in such instances, transcend bureaucratic determination of group interests.
9. Right to Political and Economic Liberty
   No citizen should be obliged, either by taxation, by regulation, or as a condition of employment, to support candidates, organizations or causes with which he disagrees. Government resources ought not underwrite policy advocacy or political activity.
10. Right to Self-Government
    Grants of power from the people to their government should be so limited and carefully prescribed as to assure that such power will be exercised in behalf of those from whom it is derived, rather than to serve those in whom it is concentrated. The vast power of the Federal bureaucracy should be dismantled, with control over public policy and government spending returned to elected officials at the local level. Local self-government, in small communities where property ownership is widespread, encourages the existence of an independent, self-determining citizenry, whose diverse control over their own affairs is itself a check on the arbitrary power of distant bureaucrats.

                                                                 (undated flyer of TCC)

On the basis of its principles, TCC is involved in pressuring and lobbying the Congress and administrations to support or oppose various specific issues. For example, TCC supports the 10% flat tax, the Strategic Defense Initiative, and aid to anticommunist freedom fighters. TCC has also opposed the Panama Canal treaties, SALT II, government funding of left-wing organizations, and U.S. aid to communist nations.

In some groups, the group beliefs refer to one broad topic that is relevant to several issues. For example, the Consumer Federation of America reflects a viewpoint that favors the protection of the rights of individual consumers through the regulation of corporate activities, and the U.S. Chamber of Commerce reflects a strong belief in the character of the American free enterprise system, opposing excessive government regulation of business. Other groups' interests are formed on the basis of narrow group beliefs reflecting single issues. For example, the National Rifle Association has a strong belief in the American citizen's unrestricted right to bear arms; the National Right to Life Committee believes in the sanctity of the fetus.

Shipley (1976) classified over 300 interest groups in Great Britain into 12 subject categories, such as political, trade union, consumer, social, religious and ethical, or environmental groups. Each group has a defined goal that may be considered as a group belief. Thus, for example, the goal of the British Measure Group is to conserve imperial measures; the goal of the Anti-Apartheid Movement is to end all British collaboration with the regime of South Africa; and the goal of the Royal Society for the Protection of Birds is to ensure the better protection of birds by developing public interest in them and in their place in nature.

Group Ideology

One of the most discussed concepts for describing a group's uniqueness is ideology. Ideology is often referred to as the mental characteristic of a group. Indeed, various definitions of ideology refer to its commonality—a state indicating that ideological beliefs are shared by group members. It reflects their common experience and serves as a basis for group members' cooperation, morale, order, and rationale for their behavior. Ideology refers to an integrated set of beliefs constituting a program, a theory of causes and effects, and premises on the nature of man and societal order (Apter, 1964; Lane, 1962; Shils, 1968). For example, Toch (1965) defined ideology as:

> a set of related beliefs held by a group of persons. The ideology of a social movement is a statement of what the members of the movement are trying to achieve together, and what they wish to affirm jointly ... the ideology of a social movement defines the movement, and contrasts it with other movements and institutions. (p. 21)

When group members hold an ideology, it frequently serves as a group belief. By definition, it consists of a set of ideas that characterize the way in which a group posits, explains, and justifies the ends and means of its organized social actions. It usually provides an identity to group members, defines the group cohesion, and describes its exclusivity. In most cases, an identification with a specific ideology indicates a membership in a particular group (Lane, 1962).

The contents of an ideology can be political, social, or even religious. An ideology usually refers to images of the desired society and the means and conditions needed to achieve it. For example, the ideology of the *Fasci Italiani di Combattimento* (the Italian Fascist Party) placed a special emphasis on a nation or a state—the fascist state. The individuals and groups are secondary to the state, which embodies the culture and spirit of the people and is considered to be the highest and noblest value. The state provides an orientation for the individuals — it is only there that they can fulfill their identity. According to the fascist ideology, life is a continuing struggle for national supremacy. In order to achieve the nation's goals, the state has to exercise complete authority over all areas of public and private life, from the education of children to control of the economy. The state has the right to control and restructure the society. Accordingly, the state requires total loyalty. There is no place for groups or individuals to object, since the state is the source of political, economic, and moral action (Mussolini, 1935). These principles served as group beliefs of the Italian Fascist Party, and, with its ascendence to power in 1922, the party tried to turn them into group beliefs for the entire nation.

For seven decades, the principles of the communist ideology have served as group beliefs especially for the members of the Communist Party of the Soviet Union, but probably also as a unique characteristic for the population of the country. This ideology is the official creed and the most accessible characteristic in every domain of life in Russia. The basic principles of communism are inculcated in the Soviet citizens from the early years of education and maintained through all the state communication channels. The ideology advocates a classless social system of equality for all members of society, which provides everyone with material and cultural benefits according to their growing needs (Triska, 1962).

In sum, this limited review of the contents did not exhaust all possible categories of group beliefs. As indicated, group beliefs can have any contents, and the above categories serve only as relevant examples of the ones that are frequently used by social scientists. Group members share group beliefs that characterize them and differentiate them from other groups. As illustrations of possible contents, this review was not based on group members' reports to identify their group beliefs, though it is possible that they actually serve as group beliefs. Future research should treat the formal statements as hypotheses that need to be validated through empirical evidence.

Characteristics of Group Beliefs

Group beliefs, as a category of beliefs, can be characterized by the same features as other beliefs. However, it is possible to focus on their unique characteristics within each of these features. Also, it should be noted that since individuals learn these beliefs, they differ with regard to the way they are adopted. Therefore, we can only discuss average characteristics of group members, which may provide an indication of how group beliefs are held.

Confidence

Group beliefs are usually held with great confidence because they are considered to be facts and verities. This occurs because group beliefs define the essence of the group and thus the reality of the individuals who view themselves as group members. In fact, in most cases, individuals voluntarily join groups, such as religious denominations, political organizations, or professional associations, on the basis of group beliefs. The act of joining a group indicates that group members accept, at least formally, group beliefs and hold them as valid.

A reduced confidence in group beliefs may shatter group members' reality, especially in cases when group membership is very important for individuals or when the change is sudden. The questioning of group beliefs, especially central ones, may have significant implications for group life. Moving group beliefs from the status of verities to the status of hypotheses may change the essence of the group or its raison d'être, or even cause its division or disintegration. It is, therefore, not surprising that groups often use various mechanisms to maintain high confidence in group beliefs.

It is recognized, though, that groups differ with regard to their insistence on confidence. While orthodox groups insist on high confidence in group beliefs (Deconchy, 1984), other groups may be less strict on this matter. The former groups do not allow any doubts or sanction their expression. The other groups are more tolerant of changes and therefore their group beliefs may be gradually altered.

Centrality

The centrality of group beliefs implies that they are often accessible in group members' repertoire and that they are relevant for consideration in making various evaluations, judgments, or decisions, including behaviors (Bar-Tal, D., 1986). The centrality characteristic of group beliefs has at least two different aspects. First, the characteristic may refer to the importance of the set of beliefs for the group members, and second, it may refer to the importance of the specific belief within the set of group beliefs.

The former aspect is based on an assumption that some groups are more important for their members than others. Individuals are usually members in a number of groups and not all of them are of equal importance to them. The importance of the group for group members is reflected in the centrality of group beliefs. That is, when the group is important for group members, in most cases the group beliefs are central. For example, it can be assumed that group beliefs are very central in groups such as the Amish (Hostetler, 1968) and Lubovitcher Hassidim (Levy, 1975). Group membership in these groups is the most important characteristic for the members, and the group beliefs are frequently accessible and often taken into consideration. In other groups, group beliefs may be unimportant for most of the group members.

The other aspect of characterizing group beliefs as central refers to the assumption that not all beliefs are of equal centrality. Some group beliefs may be of greater importance than others and thus may be more central. It means that when a group has a set of elaborated group beliefs, some of them contribute more to the group characterization and its definition than others. *The more central group beliefs are considered as prototypic in group characterization and therefore are called basic group beliefs*. Their weight in defining the essence of the group is crucial. Beyond the simple self-definition "We are a group," these beliefs provide the group's credo. For instance, in certain groups, group beliefs that refer to group goals or identity may be more central than group beliefs that refer to values or group history. In a specific example, it may be assumed that while the Mormons have numerous group beliefs, one of the basic ones is the conviction that the Book of Mormon is another Testament of Jesus Christ, a religious and secular record of ancient American civilization (O'Dea, 1957).

The centrality characteristic is not a given, but often is maintained by external factors. Availability and saliency of group beliefs in the group members' environment may influence their centrality. The first element refers to the frequency with which the content of group beliefs is exposed to group members. The other element expresses the prominence and vividness of the group belief when it is presented to group members. When group beliefs are repeatedly presented to group members in a prominent and vivid manner, they are often accessible in group members' repertoires (Higgins & King, 1981). Groups often keep group beliefs accessible by constantly repeating the contents of group beliefs. Moreover, they develop cultural and educational mechanisms to maintain group beliefs as central.

Functionality

Group beliefs are functional for an individual and a group. There are numerous functions that they can fulfill, but the two most important ones, which are implied by the definition, are identification and information.

Identification function. Group beliefs serve the function of identification. That is, group beliefs provide the basis for group membership. Individuals regard group beliefs as characterizing them as group members and as defining the boundary of the group. Group beliefs unite group members by defining the identity of the group and serving as one of the bases that allows a categorization of individuals as group members (Wilder, 1986). On this basis, individuals perceive themselves and are perceived by others as a group. Thus, on the one hand, group beliefs that serve the function of identification unify group members, and, on the other hand, these beliefs differentiate them from out-groups. The unification is reflected in the recognition of similarity (see, for example, Bar-Tal, D., 1989b). Group members are aware that they share the same beliefs that define their "groupness" and thus become aware of the similarity. Moreover, the contents of group beliefs also point out the similarities among them. Common history, common characteristics, and common needs are only a few examples of such contents. In turn, the perception of similarity may be an important source of attraction for individuals to become group members (Cartwright, 1968). Group members who differ with regard to many characteristics hold the same group beliefs, which provides a common basis. In this respect, group beliefs enhance integration and feelings of solidarity and minimize differences by focusing on commonalities and allegiance.

Also, since in many cases, groups try to be differentiated, group beliefs often provide a criterion for differentiation. Group beliefs draw the line between the in-group and out-groups. They indicate that those who do not hold the group beliefs are different. As Sherif (1951) pointed out,

> From the pointed view of inter-group relations, the most important consequence of
> group structuring is the delineation of *in-group* from *out-groups*. The development
> of in-group and "we-experience" is accompanied by the demarcation and setting of
> boundaries form outgroups. (p. 395)

In this context, we can understand Tajfel's statement: "We are what we are because
they are not what we are" (Tajfel, 1979, p. 183).

Tajfel himself made a major contribution to understanding the differentiation
process. He showed that even in the experiments using random, accidental, and
superficial criteria for group formation, subjects tried actively to differentiate
between their own and the other group (Tajfel, 1978). Thus, for example, studies by
Tajfel, Flament, Billig, and Bundy (1971), Billig and Tajfel (1973), and Allen and
Wilder (1975) showed that mere categorization of persons into groups, even on the
basis of an arbitrary task such as preferences for paintings, is sufficient for formation of the group belief "We are a group" and causes discrimination in favor of in-
group members at the expense of the out-group. The experiment by Allen and
Wilder demonstrated that group formation (including the formation of a group
belief) is a more potent factor in discrimination against out-group than the awareness that the out-group members have some similar beliefs. Also, belief similarity
about the basis for group classification (i.e., formation of a group belief) had a significant effect on discriminative behavior. Special in-group favoritism was displayed
when the in-group had similar beliefs. It thus is not surprising that the review of
intergroup relations by Brewer (1979) indicates that the need to differentiate
between in-group and out-group is a well-established phenomenon. The present
framework suggests that group beliefs foster the differentiation process.

Informative function. Group beliefs also have an informative function. First of all,
group beliefs allow the organization of the social world with the categories about the
group. They enable group members to know *what* makes them unique and different
from the out-groups. Moreover, group beliefs may provide the structure with which
group members can organize their knowledge about their own group. They provide
the raison d'être for the group and specify knowledge about various contents, such
as group history and group goals. Thus, group beliefs allow an understanding of the
group's past and of its present bonds, and possibly predict the group's future course
of action.

In cases when group beliefs are central and refer to the totality of life, they serve
as a single criterion for structuring stored knowledge and incoming information. In
this situation, group beliefs shape group members' reality and serve as a frame of
reference for organizing any knowledge. Turner and Killian (1957) noted that, in
this case, a group completely takes over the individual. An individual's perspective
stems directly from group beliefs. Group beliefs provide the entire outlook for the
world. The group commands the total allegiance of its members, and group beliefs
serve as lenses through which the world is interpreted.

In addition, specific contents may serve other functions as well. For example, as
will be presented later, group beliefs of prejudice and delegitimation, which lead to
discrimination of another group, may fulfill a function of establishing one group's

superiority over another group (see Bar-Tal, D., 1989c). Conversely, group beliefs indicating that the rest of the world has negative behavioral intentions toward that group may prepare group members for the worst and enable group members to take a course of action without considering the reaction of other groups (Bar-Tal, D., 1986). Other beliefs may serve such needs as security or self-respect (Bar-Tal, D., 1989a; Toch, 1965).

In a specific example, Simpson (1955) pointed out that the group belief of the Ras Tafari movement played several important functions in the life of the blacks in Jamaica. They provided

> compensation for the humiliation and deprivation of a lowly social station; emotional warmth and friendship of the leader and like-minded believers; hope for a better life in the other-world; recreation; opportunities for self-expression through singing, speech-making, processing-leading, and costume-wearing, recognition through office-holding, or as a speaker, musician, organizer or fund-raiser; and economic assistance at such critical times as serious illness, death in the family, and court trials. (p. 170)

Also, in the case of the Ku Klux Klan, Vander Zanden (1960) noted that the Klan's group beliefs offer the members a chance to acquire importance, hope, a sense of worthiness, meaningfulness, and purposiveness.

The above-described characteristics of group beliefs are not stable. They may change from time to time or from situation to situation. First of all, the available repertoire of group beliefs of any group is not stable. Groups add and omit group beliefs throughout their history. Second, the level of confidence, centrality, and functionality of specific group beliefs may change. Thus, group beliefs which are considered as facts may turn into doubts, while previously considered hypotheses may change into verities of group beliefs. Also, central group beliefs may turn into peripheral beliefs, and vice versa. Finally, the functions that specific group beliefs serve may also alter. The issues of change in group beliefs will be discussed further in Chapter 6.

Summary

Group beliefs can be of any content, since the numerous human groups differ in their experiences, composition, goals, structure, and environment in which they act. Indeed, the provided examples of group beliefs illustrate the variety of possible contents. Social scientists have used concepts to describe groups, but none of them corresponds to the proposed concept of group beliefs. Groups have beliefs pertaining to norms, values, goals, or ideology, but not all of them are necessarily group beliefs. Some beliefs of norms, values, goals, and ideology may characterize groups, may be shared by group members who are aware of this, and may therefore be group beliefs.

Group beliefs can be characterized not only by content, but also by psychological properties, which may change with time. First, they can be characterized by the confidence that group members attribute to them. Although most of them are treated as verities and groups use mechanisms to maintain their validity among group members, groups differ with regard to their insistence on confidence. Second, group beliefs can be characterized by their centrality, that is, in the extent of their accessibility in group members' repertoire and their relevancy for various considerations that group members make in their decisions. Group beliefs not only differ in their centrality of group members' repertoire as a whole characterizing set, but specific beliefs may also be more or less central (i.e., prototypic) in the set itself. Finally, group beliefs may be characterized by the functions that they fulfill for the group members. Although group beliefs may serve different group functions, the present analysis focused on two major functions: the identification and the informative functions. The former defines the identity of the group and the latter provides information about the group. Through the two functions group beliefs play an important if not a crucial role, in group formation and existence. These latter issues of formation and maintenance of group beliefs are discussed in Chapter 5.

Chapter 5

Formation and Maintenance of Group Beliefs

In the previous chapters, it has been established that an existence of a group indicates that group members share at least one fundamental group belief—"We are a group"—and almost always add additional group beliefs. Sharing these beliefs serves as an important characteristic of group membership. Thus, the next necessary step in the present conception is to examine the conditions and processes regarding the formation and maintenance of group beliefs.

Formation of the Fundamental Group Belief

The crucial phase in the formation of group beliefs is the emergence of the group belief indicating group existence (i.e., "We are a group"). This phase is preceded by various social perceptual and cognitive processes. According to the present view, numerous reasons can cause individuals to start believing that they constitute a group. *Individuals usually have to formulate at least one preceding belief that provides the antecedent for a group belief stating that a group exists (i.e., "We are a group").* Such an antecedent belief may later become a group belief.

Any belief can serve as an antecedent for individuals to begin considering themselves members of a group. The belief "We are a group" may be instigated by any of the following beliefs: "We act interdependently," "We have the same fate," "We have the same characteristic," "We live in the same place," "We have the same goal," "We believe in the same religious doctrine," "We have the same ancestors," "We accept the same ideology," "We are treated in the same way," and others. The antecedent belief(s) may be formed on the basis of actual experience and perception or on the basis of reliance on sources that propagate these beliefs. In the first case, individuals may actually become aware of the similarity in what may be called natural evolvement, whereas in the other case, an epistemic source may indicate to the individuals that they are similar and point out that similarity.

For example, Epstein's (1978) work indicates that ethnic identity is based on shared beliefs in common attitudes or property, which differentiate the group from the out-groups. The shared beliefs are products of common perceptions of a group's past and interaction between forces operating within a group and those coming from out-groups. Tajfel (1981) hypothesized that minority groups tend to emerge as a result of common attitudes or treatment by the outside groups that, on the one hand, facilitates the perception of a common fate, and, on the other hand, indicates the boundaries operating between the in-group and the out-groups. Several other conceptions stress individuals' shared needs (e.g., Killian, 1964; Toch, 1965), such as common feelings of frustration, alienation, deprivation, exploitation, and injustice, any of which may serve as a basis for group formation.

An experiment by social psychologists Zander, Stotland, and Wolfe (1960) may be seen as a demonstration of how the basic group belief is formed. In this experiment, the investigators created a group composed of female college students. To foster a group entity, the experimenter created conditions that provided several antecedent beliefs regarding similarity, proximity, common goals, and identity. Specifically, the experimenter systematically manipulated the perception of "groupness" by varying seating arrangements (creating proximity), by pointing to similarities among group members (creating commonality), and by assigning a goal for the group (creating competition against another group). Group members were then asked to choose a name for their group. These antecedent beliefs, together with the name of the group, produced the basic group belief "We are a group." The study also showed that these individuals behaved as group members. Thus, the investigators concluded that when a group is formed, large proportions of the self "become involved in the group and are affected by identification with the group" (p. 475).

In this vein, it is relevant to note the observation by Sherif (1936) who suggested that

> when we are in a situation with other people, our experience and subsequent behavior are modified by the special social conditions around us. The social situation may develop into some form of closed system, with more or less rigid boundaries in which the experience and actions of the individual are regulated by his membership character and his special position in the group. . . . The slogans and values that develop or become standardized in the group situation become his guides to action. (pp. 84–85)

The effects of group experiences on the formulation of the fundamental group belief are underlaid by the process of perception. It has been suggested that principles of perceptual organization contribute greatly to the self-perception of individuals as a group (Asch, 1952; Campbell, 1958). Specifically, Campbell proposed the use of four Gestalt principles (proximity, similarity, common fate, and pregnance) to explain why individuals begin to see themselves as one entity. These principles, which lead discrete elements to be perceived as parts of a whole, can be viewed as characteristics of individuals, therefore allowing definition of the group and differentiation between the in-group and the out-groups. Indeed, the review of Brewer (1979) about group formation under limited conditions indicates that factors such as interdependence, intragroup similarity, or shared fate affect the feeling of "groupness." Moreover, these factors not only determined group formation, but also influenced group members' behavior in their direction of in-group bias.

A somewhat similar approach to group formation was recently suggested by social cognitive psychologists. They placed their focus on the knowledge that individuals possess (e.g., Pryor & Ostrom, 1987). Thus, information about the collective of individuals (i.e., their attributes) serves as a basis for their self-classification as group members. This information denotes the similarity of group members and their uniqueness in comparison to out-group members.

A recent conception by Moreland (1987) extended the perceptual-cognitive perspective to four different bases for self-classification of individuals as group members, and, therefore, for the formation of the fundamental group belief "We are a group." One basis derives from the conditions and resources in the environment. Factors such as money, time, propinquity, or social networks may affect group formation. For example, people who live or work in close proximity may form a group that can be based on common goals or common interests. Also, a social network of relationships may facilitate group formation as it happens among friends or members of professional organizations.

Behavioral basis is evident when people become dependent on one another for the satisfaction of their needs. Various theoretical approaches such as evolutionary perspective, social exchange theory, social evaluation perspective, or psychodynamic theories suggest that individuals form groups in order to satisfy their various needs. Needs of survival, defense, social support, predictability, world understanding, uncertainty reduction, anxiety avoidance, or personal adjustment are only a few examples of needs that can be satisfied through group membership.

Groups may also be formed on the basis of affection as reflected in shared feelings. The positive feelings can be expressed in interpersonal attraction of group members, attraction toward group goals or activities, and love and respect of the group's leader.

Finally, the cognitive basis indicates that groups are formed when people realize that they share important personal characteristics such as attitudes, values, interests, or goals. Summarizing this basis, Moreland (1987) pointed out that

> research on personal factors suggests that small groups will form when people (a) have acknowledged their shared characteristics before, or (b) have done so recently, or (c) have found it useful to think of themselves in that way. Research on situational factors suggests that small groups will form when (d) people are reminded of shared characteristics, or (e) their outcomes seem to depend on those characteristics, or (f) the characteristics that they share are unusual in some way. (p. 103)

On the basis of the present analysis, it becomes obvious that *social categorization is the psychological process that underlies group formation in the minds of the individuals who are group members*. Tajfel's theory of social identity (1978, 1981) elaborates on this process. Social identity, which denotes a person's membership in social groups, is defined as a "part of the individual's self concept which derives from their knowledge of their membership in a social group (or groups) together with the value and emotional significance attached to that membership" (Tajfel, 1981, p. 255). The theory explaining the development of social identity suggests that social categorization provides an important basis for the group member's self-identification because group members derive aspects of their self-concepts from the social groups to which they belong. That is, once group beliefs are formed and the group is established, group members are motivated to achieve and maintain positive self-esteem. Since their evaluations depend in part on their evaluations of the group to which they belong, they are motivated to perceive their own group in positive terms. This is done by differentiating their own group from other groups on the basis of group beliefs and by perceiving their own group as superior.

More recently, Turner (1987), on the basis of social identity theory, further elaborated on the process of group formation within the framework of self-categorization theory. According to Turner, in order for a group to become a reality, a collective of individuals must group themselves cognitively as the same, in contrast to some other classes of collectives. Thus, this theory suggests that the necessary and sufficient condition for psychological group formation is social categorization. Turner hypothesizes

> that any collection of individuals in a given group setting is more likely to categorize themselves as a group (become a psychological group) to the degree that the subjectively perceived differences between them are less than the differences perceived between them and other people (psychologically) present in the setting (i.e., as the ratio of intergroup to intragroup differences increases). (These comparisons will be made on relevant dimensions selected from the common features of the self-category that includes all that are being compared). (p. 52)

The categorization process is facilitated by such factors as sharing common fate, similarity of attitudes or values, and common enemy. The internalization of the newly formed category subscribes to the principles of changing attitudes and beliefs. Later, social categorization of individuals as group members leads to coordinated behavior, shared attitudes, mutual attraction, etc.

Turner reviews several studies that provide support for his propositions. These studies demonstrate that, in the process of comparing themselves to others, individuals form a psychological group solely on the basis of shared social category. In these experiments, performed within the framework of Tajfel's social identity theory and Turner's self-categorization theory, individuals were categorized as group members and they acted accordingly (e.g., Billig & Tajfel, 1973; Hogg & Turner, 1985; Tajfel, Flament, Billig, & Bundy, 1971; Turner, Sachdev, & Hogg, 1983).

In a study by Tajfel et al. (1971), mentioned earlier, individuals were divided into groups on the basis of a fairly trivial task (expressing a preference for abstract paintings of Klee and Kandinsky or guessing the number of dots in rapidly projected clusters). Later, they were put in individual cubicles and asked to divide points worth money between two persons who were identified as either belonging to their group or not. This minimal group situation was enough to produce in-group favoritism. Individuals tended to award more points to members of their group. These results were replicated in the experiment by Billig and Tajfel (1973), when the division into groups was done on the basis of the toss of a coin.

Similarly, Wilder's (1978) experiments showed that a mere division of individuals into groups affects their cognitive, emotional, and behavioral reactions. The formation of a group reality, "We are a group," was enough for individuals to assume that they were relatively similar to one another and dissimilar to the out-group members.

Furthermore, this group belief ("We are a group") affected group members' memory—they remembered better the information that emphasized in-group similarities than out-group dissimilarities. Finally, group members favored the in-group over out-groups on trait ratings and reward distributions.

In another study by Turner, Sachdev, and Hogg (1983), school adolescents were classified into two separate groups either on the basis of random assignment or on the basis of ostensibly predetermined mutual liking or disliking. The dependent variable was distribution of points that reflected in-group favoritism. The result showed that even individuals who were categorized as a group on the basis of consensual dislike exhibited group behavior similarly to individuals categorized as a group on the basis of mutual liking. Thus, according to Turner et al., the mere categorization of individuals belonging to the same group, even when they dislike each other, leads to group formation.

In this vein, Horwitz and Rabbie (1989) suggested that external labeling is only one possible factor affecting social categorization. Moreover, on the basis of Lewin's (1948) and Sherif's (1966) conceptions, Horwitz and Rabbie suggest that social categorization is only a phase in group formation (i.e., a formation of a social category). The necessary condition for group formation is a development of interdependence. That is, a group is formed when group members become aware of their positive interdependence to one another at least in some of their goals, interests, and outcomes. This can take place when individuals expect or actually experience positive or negative consequences solely as a functional unit, a social group. According to the present framework, the group belief "We are a group" is only the first of many possible beliefs. Clearly, groups form many, often even complex group beliefs, as interdependence is formed and interaction takes place.

Still, the important contribution of minimal in-group situations to the understanding of group formation is the demonstration that the perception of the group as an entity does not have to be based on actual experiences, but a mere piece of information may be a sufficient condition for self-labeling as a group. Individuals may be told that they are given the same label (or category), and this information may cause them to form the belief "We are a group" (e.g., Billig & Tajfel, 1973). In real life situations, information or beliefs formulated by an individual (or a collective) may influence many individuals to form a new shared reality. This shared reality may serve as a basis for group formation.

Numerous political parties, religious groups, and volunteer organizations are based on group beliefs that were formulated before the group was formed. *In this process, the beliefs are first formulated, and then an attempt is made (sometimes it is even unintentional) to form a group in which these beliefs serve as group beliefs.* The following examples illustrate this process:

The Jehovah's Witness group was founded in 1872 by Charles Taze Russell in a suburb of Pittsburgh, Pennsylvania. Russell, who was brought up as a Presbyterian, was exposed to ideas of Adventism and Second Adventism until he formulated his own beliefs. These beliefs, which were later developed and modified by his successor, Joseph Franklin Rutherford, originally served as a basis for the formation of a new denomination (Stroup, 1945).

Amnesty International was initiated by Peter Benenson, who, after reading about two Portuguese students who were arrested because of toasting freedom, approached Eric Baker, a prominent Quaker, and Louis Bloom-Cooper, the internationally known lawyer, to begin a campaign to appeal for amnesty in 1961. They formulated a statement proposing

> to work impartially for the release of those imprisoned for their opinion, to seek for them a fair trial, to enlarge the right of asylum, to help political refugees find work, and to urge the creation of effective international machinery to guarantee freedom of opinion.

The group publicized the fate of eight political prisoners as its first act, and the response was overwhelming. The organization was set on the basis of the formulated principles. Sympathizers living nearby were put in contact and asked to "adopt" individual political prisoners. British artist Diana Redhouse designed an emblem for the organization based on a candle encircled by barbed wire, and the name Amnesty International was adopted (Power, 1981).

Cannon (1973) described how the Black Panthers formulated their group beliefs:

> One afternoon in October, 1966, Huey told Bobby Seale, "We need a program. We have to have a program for the people. A program that people can understand. A program that they can read and see, and which expresses their desires and needs at the same time." That night they sat down in the North Oakland Poverty Center, where they were working, and wrote out the 10-point program which is still the basis for all Panthers' actions. (p. 339)

The program concerned freedom for the black community, full employment, the end of exploitation, decent housing, true education, the exemption of blacks from military service, the end of police brutality, freedom to black prisoners, establishment of black courts, and self-determination (Cannon, 1973).

Toch (1965) presented the description of how the Anti-Digit Dialing League (ADDL) was started:

> The Anti-Digit Dialing League started over a cup of coffee in San Francisco when the conversation, quite by accident, drifted to the new Digit Dialing system. Both coffee drinkers had found the new system extremely confusing and difficult to use. They also wondered whether the change was really necessary. As a consequence they inserted a tiny notice in the classified section of a newspaper inquiring whether other people had experienced the same thoughts. They signed the ad, Anti-Digit Dialing League.
>
> The response was incredible. Over thirty-five hundred people responded within ten days in the San Francisco Bay area alone. As word about ADDL spread throughout the country, people wrote in wanting to start chapters of ADDL in other cities across the country. It quickly became obvious that ADDL was expressing a deep but previously unorganized concern of telephone users that the telephone company had somehow forgotten about them. This is the reason that ADDL started; it was an expression of widespread concern. (Toch, 1965, pp. 16–17, copied from *Phones are for People*, Anti-Digit Dialing League, 1962)

It should be noted that in all of these cases, a priori formulated beliefs have to appeal to individuals' needs in order to become a basis for group formation. It can be assumed that only then will individuals react to the formulated beliefs and join an emerging group.

Formation of Additional Group Beliefs

Once the fundamental group belief "We are a group" is formed, other group beliefs are usually added, though the contents of some additional group beliefs may be also formed as antecedent beliefs prior to the formation of the fundamental group belief. As already indicated, the contents of group beliefs can be of various categories and have unlimited scopes. Groups differ with regard to the repertoire of group beliefs that they form. They differ in the contents and in the quantity of group beliefs that they have. Each group has its own set of group beliefs. Although groups may have similar group beliefs, two separate groups must have at least one different group belief that makes them different. With regard to quantity, groups may have few group beliefs or a very long list of group beliefs. The selection of group beliefs depends very much on a group's goal(s), common experiences, ideas regarding symbols, emerging norms and values, constructed rationalizations for group formation, perceived similarities, perceived uniting forces, and so on.

One of the few studies of small groups from which the emergence of group beliefs can be inferred is the study of norm formation by Sherif (1936). He found that a group of strangers facing ambiguous stimuli tended to converge their judgments into a uniform norm. That is, common experience in a group situation served as a basis for establishing a common social reality. Sherif concluded from these results that individuals who are in contact in a defined place form common values or norms as a basis for group formation. It may be further assumed that some of these norms and values may serve as group beliefs, since they may characterize the group and underlie its uniqueness. In this line are findings obtained by Festinger and Thibaut (1951), who observed that "belonging to the same group tends to produce changes in opinions and attitudes in the direction of establishing uniformity with the group" (p. 92).

Another line of research by Sherif and his colleagues that contributes to the understanding of group belief formation is the Robber Cave experiments, which investigated intergroup conflict and cooperation (Sherif, M., Harvey, White, Hood, & Sherif, C.W., 1961). The experiments also studied the formation of a group. In one of them, 22 fifth graders were randomly divided into two groups and brought to separate camps so that group formation would be the consequence of the bonding process within the in-group without the contact of an out-group. Within 7 to 8 days the formation of the two groups emerged and stabilized. As a point of interest, it can be noted that the two groups formed various group beliefs that defined their uniqueness and character. Thus, for example, the first group selected the name "Tom Hale Rattlers," chose a flag, referred to several places as their territory, and developed a norm of "toughness" (reflected in cursing and avoidance of reporting injuries). The second group called itself "Eagles," selected their own song, and selected places in their territory for a campfire and swimming hole.

As Sherif et al. (1961) pointed out, these beliefs were produced from scratch. They were formed as a consequence of the interaction processes found in intragroup relations. They served as unique characteristics of the group and defined the substance of the "groupness." The particular group name, the flag, the norm, or the territory, in addition to the belief "We are a group," defined the essence of the group. For group members, these group beliefs served as a cognitive basis for their feeling of "groupness." The belief that they were a group, as well as other group beliefs, became part of their reality. It can be said that although the mere division into groups created the fundamental group belief, the addition of group beliefs not only strengthened the group identity, but also provided meaning to the "we-ness" reality.

A classic study by Festinger, Riecken, and Schachter (1956) on individuals' behavior in social movements that results in unfulfilled prophecies provides another example of group beliefs. In the specific case described, a housewife named Marian Keech claimed that she received a message from a superior being on another planet, stating that a flood would destroy part of the continent, including the town in which she lived. Mainly on the basis of a belief in this message, but also on the basis of the belief that she had received a communication from creatures from outer space, various individuals joined her and her main follower, Dr. Thomas Armstrong, in another town. The individuals around Mrs. Keech and Dr. Armstrong perceived themselves as a group. Their beliefs about the coming disaster and outer space communications defined their uniqueness and provided the psychological basis for group formation. They defined the essence of the group and, therefore, were group beliefs. These beliefs differentiated the members of this group from other individuals in the community who did not join the group.

In the present conception, an important question should be asked: *Which common beliefs (i.e., shared beliefs by group members) become group beliefs?* In principle, many beliefs can become group beliefs in the group members' repertoire. In reality, however, relatively few beliefs achieve this status. Three conditions are suggested as an explanation of which shared beliefs become group beliefs. One condition refers to the functionality of group beliefs. *Beliefs that are functional for group formation and maintenance become group beliefs, since it is assumed that the need to belong and the need to form social identity are important needs that underlie human beings' cognitions and behaviors.* In this context, of special importance are beliefs that differentiate the in-group and out-groups, since they allow demarcation of the group boundary and provide significant information about the group.

The differentiating beliefs indicate the similarity of group members, which overrides the differences between them. That is, through the psychological process of categorization, group beliefs simultaneously make the group members uniquely similar, yet distinctively different from members of other groups. They provide the individuals with a system of orientation toward their own group and other groups. This system leads to the perception and judgment of individuals of the same category as more similar to one another than they really are and enhances the perceptual and judgmental contrast between individuals not belonging to this category (Tajfel, 1978, 1981). An experiment by Allen and Wilder (1979) demonstrated this phenomenon. They created two groups, ostensibly on the basis of artistic preferences (which served as group beliefs), and then had group members complete an opinion survey in the manner they thought another member of their own (or the other) group would respond to the items. They found that individuals assumed that another member of their group would express beliefs more similar to their own (previously assessed) opinions than would an out-group member. This difference occurred even for belief items irrelevant to art.

In addition, those beliefs that provide information about the group become group beliefs. It is not an accident that group beliefs consist of contents that contain such elements as group history, group goals, and common characteristics of the group. These contents provide information for group members about themselves and their commonalities. They provide the raison d'être for group formation and, later, for group maintenance. Also, a fulfillment of additional functions by a belief may especially strengthen its status as a group belief. Thus, for example, beliefs that help to achieve group goals, raise the self-esteem of the group members, or strengthen the feelings of security are likely to become group beliefs.

Another condition pertains to the saliency of the beliefs that become group beliefs. Beliefs' saliency refers to those beliefs that draw special attention of group members because of prominence and distinctiveness. In combination with the first condition, these beliefs are efficiently and swiftly absorbed, and demarcate the boundary between the in-group and the out-groups. In some groups the salient group beliefs may pertain to the most perceivable cues, such as physical appearance. Special clothing, ornamentation, or even skin color may serve as a salient basis for defining one's own group. In other groups, salient beliefs may refer to individuals' needs (Toch, 1965), group goals, or common experiences.

Finally, in order for beliefs to become group beliefs, epistemic authorities of group members have to consider them as such and support them. Epistemic authorities are those knowledge sources who exert determinative influence on the formation of knowledge (Kruglanski, 1989). Group members attribute high confidence to beliefs coming from epistemic authority, consider these beliefs as truth, and adopt them as part of their own repertoires. In our case the concept applies mostly to leaders who perpetuate beliefs that become group beliefs. Political, intellectual, religious, social, and cultural leaders determine to a considerable extent which beliefs become group beliefs and influence group members to accept them as such. They frequently select the group's goals which may serve as group beliefs, formulate ideologies or religious doctrines, decide what events in the past should be remembered as group beliefs for the future, often select the symbols for the group, and decide on the attributes that characterize group members (e.g, Bar-Tal, Y., 1989a).

It is usually in the formative phase of group development that group beliefs are established. This is a period of malleability during which group beliefs are formulated and reformulated. With time, group beliefs emerge in a relatively stable formulation, although always with a possibility of change. In any event, as long as the group exists, it will always be faced with the task of disseminating group beliefs and maintaining them.

Dissemination of Group Beliefs

Group beliefs, which are part of individuals' cognitive repertoire, are shared by group members after being acquired through social processes. Thus, the question of the dissemination of group beliefs among the group members is important in the study of group beliefs.

Group beliefs are social products of the cognitive processes of group members. They reside in an individual's mind. The process of group belief formation begins with an individual or a group of individuals who form a group belief. Then, whether a belief is first acquired by group members and later becomes a group belief, or whether it becomes a group belief that group members later acquire as such, the process of dissemination is imperative and indispensable. Group members have to acquire and hold group beliefs. The dissemination process of group beliefs consists of two complementary parts. It not only requires the dissemination of the specific contents, but also requires that group members believe that these ideas are shared by other group members and are characteristic of them.

Ways of dissemination may differ among various groups and are also contingent on specific situations. In small groups, the dissemination process can take place via face-to-face interaction, but in large groups it may occur through mediating persons, mail, or mass media. Each group develops its own means of disseminating group beliefs using various political, societal, cultural, or educational mechanisms. Large, institutionalized groups use such channels as books, speeches of leaders, newspapers, magazines, or radio or television programs to impart group beliefs among group members. Moreover, many of the groups have institutions and authorities whose primary function is to pass group beliefs to group members. Teachers, public relations officials, information agencies, leaders, and others provide group members with information that includes group beliefs. One illustration of a specific dissemination technique can be observed in the Communist Party of the Soviet Union, which developed party schools for inculcating its ideology (i.e, group beliefs). In these schools, the cadres of the party not only learn the contents and premises of the ideology that shape their own cognitive repertoire, but they also acquire skills to work with the masses in order to spread the group beliefs (Gehlen, 1969).

An example of a theory that has relevance for the dissemination of group beliefs is the social impact theory (Latané, 1981; Latané & Wolf, 1981). On the basis of this theory, it is possible to suggest that the influence of the group on its members to accept the group beliefs depends on (a) the strength of the sources that impart these beliefs (status, power, abilities, or their level of perceived epistemic authority in general), (b) the immediacy of the sources in terms of proximity in time or space to group members, and (c) the number of sources propagating the group beliefs. It is beyond the objectives of this book to elaborate on the ways of disseminating beliefs. Nevertheless, knowledge accumulated in the literature of attitude change, compliance, and socialization provides much enlightenment on this topic.

Two previously made notes should be remembered in the discussion of the acquisition of group beliefs in the process of their dissemination. First, it should be assumed that group members, as individuals who have their own personality attri-

butes, skills, motivations, and knowledge, differ with regard to the degree of centrality that they ascribe to group beliefs. For some group members, group beliefs may
be very central, while for other group members they may be peripheral. Also, group
members differ with regard to attributing centrality to specific group beliefs. For
some group members, certain group beliefs may be more important than others.
However, a necessary condition for beliefs to become group beliefs is an agreement
among group members regarding the characterization of their "groupness." A seri-
ous disagreement among the group members regarding the nature of group beliefs
may result in a group schism. This phenomenon will be discussed later.

Second, once the group beliefs are acquired, their accessibility may change from
time to time. That is, although a group may have in its repertoire a long list of group
beliefs, not all of them have to be accessible at the same time. Different group beliefs
may appear in group members' minds in different situations, since different situations may invoke different beliefs. However, some group beliefs may be very central
for the essence of the group, and, therefore, they may be more or less constantly
accessible in each group member's repertoire.

Maintenance of Group Beliefs

Group members are expected to accept and maintain beliefs that indicate their identity. This is a fundamental requirement for group existence. The longevity of social
groups depends to some degree on the maintenance of group beliefs among group
members. Large portions of the group, and especially an influential part, must hold
group beliefs, since the group could not otherwise survive. If the confidence in
group beliefs dissipates, the group may disintegrate since an important basis, which
provided the rationale for collective existence as a group, no longer exists. Therefore, the group actively presses its members to hold and maintain group beliefs. As
Sherif (1951) noted,

> one of the products of group formation is a delineation of "we" and "they"—the
> "we" thus delineated comes to embody a whole host of qualities and values to be
> upheld, defended, and cherished. Offenses from without or deviations from within
> are promptly reacted to with appropriate corrective, defensive, and, at times, offen-
> sive measures. (p. 396)

A considerable portion of social science research has been devoted to the study of
group pressures for uniformity (e.g., Cartwright & Zander, 1968; Festinger,
Schachter, & Back, 1950; Levine, in press; Shaw, 1976; Verba, 1961). This literature can be used to explain the psychological processes whereby groups maintain
their group beliefs.

Groups differ with regard to the control mechanisms that they use to maintain
group beliefs among group members. In some groups, there are no control mechanisms. The guiding assumption in these groups is that those who join them and maintain their membership share group beliefs. However, the great majority of these
groups develop various channels of communication, which not only keep the groups

alive, but also preserve group beliefs. Thus, for example, in these groups, regular meetings, newsletters, or mass media information may remind members about the group beliefs and thus maintain them.

Other groups require adherence to group beliefs and some may even use various types of sanctions as means of control. These groups differ with regard to sanctions, which are applied to group members who do not adhere to group beliefs. Among groups that use sanctions, some sanctions might be minor and of a mainly social nature, while others might be more formal and used against group members who openly express their reservation or rejection of the group beliefs.

In the former groups, group members may express explicitly, or even implicitly, their disapproval and dissatisfaction with individuals who do not adhere to group beliefs. In the latter groups, the sanctions may consist of a reprimand or even expulsion. For example, the rules of the Communist Party of the Soviet Union passed by the 22nd Congress specificaliy refer to such sanctions. Rule 9, dealing with duties and rights of party members, reads:

> 9. A party member who fails to fulfill his duties as laid down in the Rules, or commits other offenses, shall be called to account, and may be subjected to the penalty of admonition, reprimand (or severe reprimand), with entry in the registration card. The highest Party penalty is expulsion from the Party.
>
> Should the necessity arise, a Party organization may, as a Party penalty, reduce a Party member to the status of candidate member for a period of up to one year. The decision of the primary Party organization reducing a Party member to candidate membership is subject to endorsement by the district or city Party committee. On the expiration of his period of reduction to candidate membership his readmission to full membership of the Party will follow the regular procedure, with retention of his former Party standing.
>
> In the case of insignificant offenses, measures of Party education and influence should be applied—in the form of comradely criticism, Party censure, warning, or reproof. (Triska, 1962, pp. 163–164)

Indeed, Rigby (1968) reported that expulsion was a widely used practice. For example, in 1961, Khrushchev stated that over 200,000 persons had been expelled for various reasons since 1955, but this number was only 40% of the expulsions carried out between 1951 and 1955.

The extent and intensity to which group members adhere voluntarily to group beliefs may be seen as an indication of group cohesiveness. Whereas centrality of group beliefs in group members' repertoire may indicate a high level of cohesiveness, relative disregard of group beliefs may indicate a low level of cohesiveness. That is, when there is a consensus about group beliefs and when group members frequently think about them, view them as unquestionable facts, and consider them as relevant to the decision-making process, then it can be said that the group is highly cohesive. In contrast, when there is a low consensus about group beliefs, and/or they are not considered to be important, then it can be said that the group is not cohesive. This view, in contrast to general definitions, specifies that the nature of the group members' commitment reflects the cohesiveness of the group. For example, Cartwright (1968) defined cohesiveness as the total sum of forces attracting members to a group, while Festinger (1950) suggested that cohesiveness reflects the pressure to stay in a group.

High centrality of group beliefs indicates that they are important for group members and that they satisfy their needs. When group beliefs are central, group members stay in a group and are attracted to it. It can be assumed that in this situation group members' identification with the group is high. Moreover, the belief that group beliefs are shared by the group members strengthens the feeling of "we-ness." Thus, according to the present view, group beliefs in cohesive groups express a kind of cement that binds group members together, maintains their relationship to one another, and makes them act in a coordinated manner. Parsons (1951) referred to this process as belief institutionalization. It takes place when "subscription to a system of beliefs becomes a criterion of loyalty to a collectivity, as such as a religious group" (p. 56).

Extension of Group Membership

Once the group has been established and group beliefs formulated, new members may join the group. *Although individuals join groups for various reasons, it is assumed that the act of joining a group implies at least external acceptance of group beliefs.* In principle, this is the symbolic explicit meaning of joining a group: Individuals indicate that they accept group beliefs (see Moreland & Levine, 1982). This is a process of assimilation. The new member, by accepting group beliefs, becomes similar to other group members.

Group beliefs provide the potential members with the information about the raison d'être of the group. They provide the rationale for group existence, and, as such, they often serve as the basis on which group members decide to associate. Either an agreement with group beliefs, their appeal, or identification with them may cause individuals to join the group. Other reasons are also possible. As Warriner and Prather (1965) suggested, groups may satisfy different needs for an individual. They may provide pleasure through activities, may evoke and reaffirm a valued belief system, may serve as a vehicle for desired communion with others, or may produce goods, service, or some kind of change in objects.

The procedure of accepting new members may vary in its formality. While some groups may not have any formal procedures of acceptance, other groups may have at least a formal application requirement. In the former type of group, mere participation in group activities or in communication networks indicates acceptance of group beliefs and joining the group. Other groups differ with respect to what they require from an individual for membership. Some groups require not only a formal application procedure, but also a process of learning group beliefs before they accept a person as a group member. For example, the rules of the Communist Party of the Soviet Union from 1961 describe the process of admission as follows:

> 4. Applicants are admitted to Party membership only individually. Membership in the Party is open to politically conscious and active working people devoted to the communist cause from among the workers, peasants and intellectuals. New members are admitted from among the candidate members who have passed through the established probationary period. Persons may join the Party on attaining the age of

eighteen. Young people up to the age of twenty may join the Party only through the Young Communist League (YCL).

The procedure for the admission of candidate members to full Party membership is as follows:

(A) applicants for Party membership must submit recommendations from three Party members who have a Party standing of not less than three years and who know the applicants from having worked with them, professionally and socially, for not less than one year.

(B) Application for Party membership are discussed and a decision is taken by the general meeting of the primary Party organization; the decision of the latter takes effect after endorsement by the district Party committee, or by the city Party committee in cities with no district divisions. . . .

14. All persons joining the Party must pass through a probationary period as candidate members in order to familiarize themselves with the Program and Rules of the CPSU and prepare for admission to full membership of the Party. Party organizations must assist candidates to prepare for admission to full membership of the Party, and test their personal qualities. Probationary membership shall be one year. [Cf. Art. 18, 1952 Rules.]

15. The procedure for the admission of candidate members (individual admission, submission of recommendations, decision of the primary organization as to admission, and its endorsement) is identical with the procedure for the admission of Party members.

16. On the expiration of a candidate member's probationary period the primary Party organization discusses and passes a decision on his application for admission to full membership. Should a candidate member fail, in the course of his probationary period, to show his worthiness, and should he prove, by his personal qualities, to be unfit for admission to membership in the CPSU, the Party organization shall pass a decision rejecting his admission to membership in the Party; after endorsement of that decision by the district or city Party committee, he shall cease to be considered a candidate member of the CPSU.

(Triska, 1962, pp. 160–161, 166–168)

In the same vein, Galanter (1980) described the recruitment process of new members to the Unification Church (the members of which are called "Moonies"). In this process, considerable effort is directed at presenting and imparting group beliefs. In a series of lectures, the potential members are exposed to the group beliefs and later evaluated, among other things, on the extent to which they accept these beliefs. Only on the basis of the evaluation are individuals later accepted as group members.

In many cases, groups actively try to recruit members. They search for individuals who may accept the group beliefs and become group members. Groups such as religious denominations, sects, political parties, or various other voluntary organizations make efforts to convince individuals of the validity, importance, and utility of their group beliefs. Moreover, some of the groups have special institutions and even specialists who function to attract new members for the group.

Nevertheless, not all the groups are open and accept new members on the basis of their acceptance of group beliefs. Some groups have group beliefs that limit group membership to specific categories of individuals. These restrictive beliefs can pertain to characteristics such as sex, race, ethnic origin, religion, geographical residence, or even particular experience. For example, the Order of the Sons of Italy in America is limited to members who are of Italian descent and live in the United States; the

National Black Sisters' Conference restricts its membership to black Catholic women; and the Society of Vietnamese Rangers is limited to ranger, paratroopers, and commandos who were advisors to fighting parties in South East Asia.

Finally, it should be noted that being a member of a group and sharing its group beliefs do not preclude the possibility of joining another group and at the same time sharing another set of group beliefs. Individuals can be members of several groups at the same time and hold several sets of group beliefs. For example, they may be members of a work group, a volunteer organization, a professional organization, a religious group, an ethnic group, and a nation. Each group has a set of group beliefs that characterizes it. In most cases, individuals are members of groups whose group beliefs do not contradict each other.

Also, membership in several groups does not imply that multiple group beliefs held by the individuals are simultaneously accessible at any given moment. We may expect that accessibility of particular group beliefs at any given moment depends on the salience of the cues of that group and the individual's attention to these cues (see Charters & Newcomb, 1952; Kelley, 1955). Thus, contingent on a specific situation and thoughts, certain group beliefs may be accessible at certain times. Such functioning facilitates multiple group membership.

Summary

On the basis of the proposed definition of a group it is suggested that group members have to share a fundamental group belief, "We are a group," to which are added other group beliefs. The formation of the fundamental group belief is based on the social, perceptual, and cognitive processes in which individuals find out about the commonality among them and categorize themselves as being group members. The fundamental belief is based on at least one preceding belief that provides the antecedent for this group belief. Subsequently, the antecedent beliefs may become additional group beliefs.

Group beliefs fulfill various needs of group members, and on their basis individuals may decide whether to join a group. They especially allow the demarcation between the group and out-groups, and construct an orientation about the group through the provided knowledge. It is therefore not surprising that group beliefs are usually salient by being prominent and distinctive. Also, group epistemic authorities support them and try to maintain them.

Group members develop various ways of disseminating group beliefs in order to consolidate group existence. They also use different mechanisms to maintain them. Some groups even resort to formal control means with sanctions in order to preserve the group. Nevertheless, group beliefs are not stable and are related to changes through which groups go. These changes are subjects of Chapter 6.

Chapter 6

Group Beliefs and Group Changes

Groups are not static entities; rather, they have dynamic natures. They constantly go through various changes regarding different aspects of their structure (e.g., cohesiveness, norms, leadership, membership composition), tasks (e.g., goals, means), or processes (e.g., communication, conformity, pressures). The inevitable changes are due to continuously shifting, external conditions to which the group must adapt, and to ongoing internal processes that involve the active nature of human beings — the groups members.

There are many ways to analyze groups' changes, and social scientists have dealt with this issue since the study of groups began (e.g., Golembiewski, 1962; Moscovici, 1976; Shaw, 1976; Verba, 1961). However, one way to approach the inquiry into group change is to focus on group beliefs. The present perspective suggests an examination of how changes in groups reflect the process of alteration within the system of group beliefs. This examination may illuminate, from a particular angle, why certain changes take place in groups' lives. This chapter will discuss such phenomena as group mergence, subgroupings, changes of group beliefs, splits (schisms), and group disintegration.

Mergence of Groups

The mergence of groups is a known phenomenon in group dynamics. Two groups, or sometimes even more, may merge to form one united group. Mergence can take place, for example, between two political parties, as happened in 1988 between the Social Democratic and Liberal Parties in Great Britain; between two interest groups, as in the 1987 case of the Committee for a Sane Nuclear Policy and the Nuclear Weapons Freeze Campaign in the United States; or between religious organizations, as in the case where three Lutheran groups decided to merge into one group in 1986, becoming the Evangelical Lutheran Church in America. *While it is recognized that the motivations to merge may be varied, it is possible to assume that the basis for mergence is almost always the result of a similarity between the group beliefs of the merging groups.* It is the similarity of group beliefs that allows the merging groups to formulate a new set of group beliefs and redefine, without much difference, a new identity for the group members. Therefore, it is probably rare that groups with contradictory or different group beliefs will merge.

Thus, one way to analyze mergence is to examine the group beliefs of the merging groups before the mergence and to follow up on the formation of their new set. This examination sheds light not only on the process of mergence (for example, which of the groups had more influence on the formulation of new group beliefs), but also on the nature of the newly emerged group. In this analysis, the first phase of merging requires the recognition by the merging groups that their group beliefs are similar. This recognition usually takes place as a result of contact through action in the same environment or through communication if the groups are based in different locales. The groups may be similar in their group beliefs pertaining to goals, values, ideology, or in other contents.

In many cases, the recognition of the similarity of the groups' beliefs leads to cooperation and coordination of activities. This is often the stage in which the two groups can examine the feasibility of mergence and evaluate its possible success. The idea of mergence usually appears in this phase. Subsequently, the process of merging may begin, assuming that the groups do not differ with regard to central group beliefs, which may preclude a mergence.

The necessary phase for mergence is the negotiation of an agreeable set of group beliefs. While the negotiation concerns many aspects of mergence, the determination of new group beliefs may be, in many cases, its essential part. Each group usually tries to transfer as many of its own group beliefs as possible to the newly formulated set. One of the final outcomes of mergence is the formation of group beliefs for the new group. These group beliefs serve as a uniting bond for members of the new group. They provide the new identity for the merged group and a new definition for the "groupness."

The mergence between the Committee for a Sane Nuclear Policy (SANE) and the Nuclear Weapons Freeze Campaign (FREEZE) is an example of the above process. SANE was established in 1957 following an advertisement that appeared in the New York Times (November 15, 1957) calling for an end to nuclear testing. With time, the group added other group beliefs that served as guides for its activities. For example, the United States' policy in Latin America became an important preoccupation of SANE in the 80s. FREEZE was established in 1980 with the purpose of urging and speeding up a freeze of the nuclear arms race. Its group belief stated a firm commitment "to the achievement of a comprehensive bilateral and verifiable freeze between the United States and the Soviet Union."

Both groups had similar group beliefs and collaborated frequently. The idea of merging was raised several times, but only in March, 1986 did the two groups begin negotiation. The newsletter of SANE, *Sane World*, of September/October, 1986, reported on the unity talks, noting the similarity between the two groups:

> Both groups have made a comprehensive test ban treaty as their number one priority in 1986. Both groups oppose Star Wars and the abandonment of SALT II. Both

groups are working for a redirection of American military policy from nuclear stockpiling and interventionism to nuclear disarmament and global peace. (p. 1)

When a 17-member commission was set up to negotiate the merger, one of the two subcommittees was specifically formed to negotiate the new set of group beliefs. This task was accomplished, and in the spring of 1987 the two groups merged. In a publication entitled *Sane/Freeze* in autumn 1987, the co-directors of the new group wrote:

> As we merge, SANE/FREEZE continues to be one of the few disarmament groups that can mobilize large numbers of its own constituents.... By merging, we are creating a new force in American policy—a large-scale peace organization with the necessary political clout and clarity of vision to make a real difference in national policy.

Subgrouping

Another widely observed phenomenon in groups is the emergence of subgrouping. *From the perspective of the present conception, this phenomenon indicates that while all group members accept the basic group beliefs, some of them form and hold additional beliefs, which unite and characterize them as a subgroup. These beliefs can be considered as subgroup beliefs, which define the "subgroupness."* In this case, the subgroup beliefs differentiate the subgroup from other members of the group. They provide the boundaries for the subgroup and indicate that those who are subgroup members subscribe to them, as well as to the basic group beliefs.

Lijphart (1975) described a special case of subgroupings in Dutch society, which is characterized by religious and class divisions. Each group not only has its own group beliefs, but also has institutions to support them. Such a fragmented system could lead to dissension and conflict in the group. Nevertheless, Holland is considered as a stable, democratic society in which potential conflicts are diffused successfully. Lijphart (1975) explained this paradox by pointing out that there is agreement on basic group beliefs. Thus, while each group tries to defend and promote its own interests, at the same time it tries to maintain the system and support the consensus. According to Lijphart, the most important Dutch group belief refers to nationalism. This belief is deeply rooted and is reflected in various symbols. Also, the great support for democratic institutions provides an important basis for unity.

Subgrouping takes place especially in large groups, such as political parties or religious denominations. In fact, several political theorists view political parties as a collection of interest subgroups, a union of small groups, or an association of communities (e.g., Duvenger, 1954; Eldersveld, 1964). However, subgrouping may also be found in relatively small groups such as small political parties or ideological groups. Groups may have few, several, or many subgroups. The contents of subgroup beliefs may consist of various topics. It may refer to goals, values, or past experiences.

In many cases, the major goal of subgroups is to change group beliefs. This is often the main reason for their emergence. In such a case, they advocate the addition, omission, or change of at least one or more group beliefs. Subgrouping, as an institutionalized mechanism, allows group members to hold a variety of beliefs and to press for changes in a group. Thus, for example, the Labor Party in Israel has a number of factions with more or less formal membership. Although these factions accept the political platform of the party formulated in general terms, they disagree about specific means, goals, or ideological dogma. In this case, the disagreements among the factions often pertain to desirable solutions to the Israeli-Arab conflict, which dominates the political arena.

Groups differ with regard to their policy of institutionalizing subgroups that focus on changing group beliefs. While some groups allow minimal divergence from group beliefs, others not only tolerate dissent, but also serve as a loose framework for subgroups with different beliefs. Nevertheless, in both cases, the basic group beliefs have to be accepted by all the group members, since they serve as a uniting bond for the subgroups. In groups in which little deviation from group beliefs is allowed, few subgroups emerge. These groups often utilize control mechanisms to keep group members in line and severely sanction any deviations. One example of such a group is the Jehovah's Witnesses. Stroup (1945), who studied this group, pointed out that

> the belief system of the Jehovah's Witnesses is totalitarian. The theology does not attempt to make a partial inquiry into the nature of reality, but claims to have succeeded already in obtaining the final answer to all important religious problems. . . . Obviously, such a rigid acceptance of dogma precludes any of the spontaneity that comes from free, creative attempts at problem solving in the religious area. The beliefs laid down by Mr. Russell and developed and modified by Mr. Rutherford still remain unchanged for the most part. . . . The whole movement has been built on authoritarian method. . . . For years hyperorthodox Witnesses have lived in an unquestioning devotion to their leader. . . . Deviations from the Rutherford gospel are reported to the central organization. . . . When heresy is reported to the central organization, the heretic is brought before a company council and is usually immediately isolated from other Witnesses. (pp. 124–125)

In groups with a democratic, tolerant climate, the emergence of subgroups is a natural phenomenon. Group members contemplate various ideas, express them, and try actively to influence the group. One way of struggling for change is to form an organization of a lobbying subgroup on the basis of newly proposed beliefs. These new beliefs may serve as the subgroup's beliefs, providing the essence of the subgroup's existence and the definition for its identity. Members can join the subgroup if they identify with the subgroup's beliefs.

Although subgrouping may also be caused by personality clashes among the leaders or by organizational discord, it is the disagreement over group beliefs that is seen in many groups as a legitimate reason for forming a subgroup. Therefore, in many groups, a formation of subgroups is always presented as a disagreement over group beliefs. Zuckerman (1979) provides an extensive analysis of subgroups within the Christian Democratic Party in Italy. These subgroups, called factions, are structured around a patron, who participates in the power struggle for the leadership and tries to extend his political resources. Nevertheless, each subgroup adds ideological slogans, which serve as subgroup beliefs and provide identity.

Subgrouping does not necessarily have to be related to goals or ideology. Subgrouping can also be based on other contents, such as past experience or ancestors. For example, Levy (1975) reported that Lubovitch Hassidim are divided into four subgroups on the basis of their past ties to the Lubovitch community. The group differentiates those who have ancestral ties to Lubovitch, those who come from orthodox Jewish families and join the Lubovitch Hassidim, those who join the group as recent converts, and those who do not necessarily observe the rituals, but feel emotionally tied to the group. This system of subgroups affects certain patterns of interaction within the community.

Subgrouping may also emerge in groups that are greatly preoccupied with shaping their group beliefs. This is especially true in groups that are in the phase of formulating their group beliefs. In these groups, if the climate allows, group members constantly formulate, reformulate, revise, and change their own beliefs until, as it sometimes happens, the climate changes and no revisions of group beliefs are encouraged. In these types of groups, subgrouping is a common phenomenon. Group members, in their attempt to influence the formulation of group beliefs, organize themselves into subgroups.

Examples of these cases can be found in small ideological groups whose members spend much energy in discussing, refining, and changing group beliefs (see Bell, 1952; Rayner, 1986). Bell, in describing the various socialist groups in the United States in the last century and the beginning of the present one, noted the extensive subgroupings involved in the definition of groups' ideologies.

In any group the number of subgroups and their size may change over time. Subgroups may merge, split, or disintegrate. These changes may take place as a function of group processes at large, such as changes in type of leadership, changes in pressure to conform, and changes in group climate. Obviously, changes with regard to group beliefs may also affect subgrouping. For example, a change of group beliefs may imply an achievement of an advocated goal and an end of the basis for the subgroup's existence. However, as long as the structure permits, groups will have subgroupings.

Change of Group Beliefs

In most groups, group beliefs change with time. The change can take place either by the addition and/or omission of beliefs or by the reformulation of the old ones. The change reflects a process of adaptation to the changing conditions in the environment and to the changing needs of group members. As an illustration, Nagata (1981) described the continuous reformulation of Malay identity in the face of immigration of Arabs and Chinese as well as religious changes. While certain beliefs characterizing Malayans (e.g., adherence to Islam) are not unique to them, other traditional characteristics are not widely shared (e.g., pattern of dress). What remained as a basic group belief is a sense of shared descent, of belonging to the same *bangsa*:

> The term bangsa conveys the double ideas of people sharing both a common origin
> and a common culture.... It has a primordial quality, for it implies that the cul-
> tural traits are inalienably and inextricably associated with a particular people, that
> is, carried by a community whose ultimate unity derives from a single origin. (p.
> 98)

The most important variable that determines whether group beliefs change and
determines the extent of any change is the climate of the group. The climate may res-
trict any innovative ideas regarding group beliefs or may be tolerant and open with
regard to these changes. An increasingly tolerant climate enables increasingly more
changes to take place. Coser (1954) described, for example, the nature of sects that
are "never tolerant," do not allow departure from group beliefs, press for uniformity,
ostracize deviants, and reward conformity.

Nevertheless, even relatively closed and authoritative groups change group
beliefs. In times of continuously changing environments, facilitated communication
among group members as well as between the in-group and out-groups, and availability of information, it is almost impossible to prevent influences that may affect
group beliefs. It is especially difficult for a group to be effectively closed to information and ideas coming from out-groups. Even if it is closed, though, the group still
must cope with environmental changes consisting of physical (e.g., technology) and
social (e.g., norms, values) aspects which may affect the mental state of the group
(Zald, 1982). Finally, to avoid changes, the group must impose complete control
over members who may produce ideas inconsistent with group beliefs. Thus, even
a relatively closed group like the Amish could not completely isolate themselves in
their environment and has had to absorb changes from out-groups. Hostetler (1968)
noted some of these influences. He wrote:

> The general influences of American culture, both material and non-material,
> gradually find their way into segments of the Amish. The methods used to keep the
> community in bounds, described earlier, are not 100 per cent effective in keeping
> the outside out. The following changes have occurred in one or more communities:
> Ball bearings have been adopted on carriage wheels. Dairy barns have been remo-
> deled to conform to standards required for selling fluid milk. The young men have
> changed from black to brown shoes. Hair is cut shorter than the previous genera-
> tion. Mothers have changed from cotton to nylon material for some women's gar-
> ments. Tractors for field work have been allowed. The trend from general to
> specialized farming is very apparent. Young men and women have become
> interested in education, in occupations other than farming, and in missionary work.
> Some Amish districts have gone so far as to allow electricity, ownership of automo-
> biles, and telephones. Kitchens have been modernized with appliances. Bottled gas
> in lieu of electricity, milking machines run by small gasoline engines, and refrigera-
> tors operated with kerosene are still other changes. The adoption of such innova-
> tions requires reintegration of culture and reorganization of values. (p. 323)

In other examples, Triska (1962) demonstrated changes in the Communist Party
of the Soviet Union's programs. Although this party was considered totalitarian and
closed, these changes inevitably lead to the modification of group beliefs. According
to Triska, in the Second Congress of the party in 1903, the formulated basic group
beliefs referred to the growing contradiction between the exploiting capitalism and

the exploited masses in bourgeois societies, which can only be resolved by social revolution. The party believed that the revolution should be carried out by the proletariat, which will overthrow the autocracy and build a democratic republic, and that the democratic republic will bring political and civil freedom, universal education, self-determination for all nationalities, election of judges, separation of church and state, and a militia in place of a standing army.

With the revolution in 1917, the new group beliefs formulated in 1919 accounted for the changes that took place. Thus, the group beliefs referred to the successful revolution and a foundation of communist society. They related to the outbreak of additional revolutions and asserted that a period of wars and imperialism was inevitable. Also, the beliefs condemned the Social Democratic and Socialist parties for opportunism. Finally, the beliefs referred to the goals of the All-Russian Communist Party. Later, in 1952, new changes came as the 19th Party Congress resolved that

> fundamental changes have taken place both in the sphere of international relations and in the sphere of the construction of socialism in the USSR, in which connection many of the propositions set forth in the Program and tasks of the Party expounded therein . . . no longer correspond to modern conditions and the Party's new tasks. (Triska, 1962, p. 6)

The new group beliefs were formulated only in 1961 and their content looks like heresy in comparison to 1919 beliefs. They advocate coexistence with imperialism, grant considerable "rights" to all Soviet people, and do not mention, for example, a militia or moneyless economy. It is possible that the new changes advocated presently by Mikhail Gorbachev will shape new group beliefs of the Soviet Communist Party.

In groups that have a formal listing of group beliefs, a change may also involve their formal reformulation, as in the previous example of the Soviet Communist Party. Such reformulation may be the first step in changing group beliefs, as an initiation of change, or it may be done in the course of the changing process. Sometimes, a formal reformulation is only a validation of an already shared belief after the group members themselves have changed the group belief. In any event, the formal change of beliefs is a symbolic act that is often important for a group's life.

Changes of group beliefs can originate from the same sources that initiate all the other changes in the group's life. Both the leader's initiatives and the minority's influence play an important role in changing group beliefs. Leaders who initiate changes and innovations may also decide to alter group beliefs. Such a move may reflect their own convictions and/or a compliance with group members' needs. The latter condition is probably necessary if group members are to adopt the change. The new group beliefs are accepted by group members to the extent that they are functional for their needs (Bar-Tal, Y., 1989b; Griffin, Skivington, & Moorhead, 1987; McCall & Lombardo, 1978). This latter condition applies to all situations of change in group beliefs. Group members' needs play a role in the acceptance of new group beliefs.

An analysis of change in group beliefs of the Woman's Christian Temperance Union (WCTU) from the 1880s to 1950s provides an example of the relationship between group members' needs and group beliefs (Gusfield, 1955). With the establishment of the group in 1874, the group beliefs mostly focused on the improvement of morality and of economic conditions of women. Specifically, the beliefs pertained to such topics as long working hours, low wages, and child labor. After 1900, while the humanitarian group beliefs regarding change in economic conditions became less central, the group beliefs concerning temperance and morality became more prominent. One example of this change was a new emphasis on the destructiveness of the drinking habit. With time, group beliefs about morality and temperance continued to gain centrality, while group beliefs of humanitarian interest lessened in importance. These changes took place because group members changed and different group beliefs appealed to different members. While in the early stages of group existence, group members were mostly from the upper middle class and were preoccupied with humanitarian beliefs; later, the membership shifted to the lower classes, who were more receptive to temperance issues.

With regard to a subgroup's attempts to change group beliefs, a recent burgeoning of work in social psychology can shed light on the conditions that facilitate minority influence (e.g., Levine & Moreland, 1985; Maass & Clark, 1984; Moscovici, 1976; Moscovici, Mugny, & Van Avermaet, 1985; Mugny, 1982). The findings of this line of research suggest the following: (a) the influence of a minority develops with time and usually is not found in the initial phases of group formation; (b) the influence of a minority often appears to be latent; (c) the influence of a minority is mediated by an innovation process that offers new ideas to group members' repertoire; (d) the influence of a minority is mostly carried out through behavioral style—in order to be effective, a minority must be consistent, coherent, and forceful, but also flexible in pressing for a change; (e) a minority will be more successful in changing group beliefs if it argues for a position in line with the general social climate of group members (i.e., the social zeitgeist); and (f) minorities are also more likely to succeed when they are similar to the majority in all respects except for the group beliefs that they are striving to change.

Any change of group beliefs requires a modification of the group members' repertoire. Group beliefs are changed when group members share the new belief and consider it as characterizing their uniqueness. This is a long gradual process that may require dissemination of the new beliefs and persuasion of group members to make the change. Group members are the ones who have to hold the new group beliefs. Only when the new beliefs are accepted and shared is the process of change completed.

Group Schism

Since splits within groups are frequently the result of disagreements over group beliefs, one way of analyzing the schism process is to focus on these beliefs. *In situations of such disagreements, some of the group members, who frequently are organized in a subgroup, try to omit, add, and/or formulate at least some of the group beliefs. When the disagreement involves the most important group beliefs and no com-*

promise can be found as a solution, then a schism may take place. The members of the subgroup then leave and form a new group with new group beliefs. An example of a split over group beliefs is the case of the Clamshell Alliance, an antinuclear protest group active in New England during the late 1970s (Downey, 1986). The Clamshell Alliance was established in July, 1976, in direct reaction to the building of the Seabrook nuclear power plant in southeastern New Hampshire. The basic beliefs of the group pertained to stopping the construction of the plant by using direct, nonviolent action as a strategy. In addition, group beliefs defined the egalitarian identity of the organization. Over time, some of the group members challenged these two main group beliefs and suggested changing the consensus decision-making process and using civil disobedience as a means for achieving the goal. Since the majority of the group members did not agree with changing these beliefs, a small part of the group members left to establish their own organization, The Coalition for Direct Action in Seabrook. The group beliefs of the new group referred to civil disobedience as a strategy in the struggle to close the plant and required a 75% majority rule to make decisions. The Clamshell Alliance continued to adhere to its nonviolent strategy, but changed the consensus principle to 90% majority rule (Downey, 1986).

Splits are not necessarily based on disagreements about group beliefs, but when this is the case, they can take place in at least one of two possible ways: (a) A subgroup may decide that it does not accept the group beliefs and therefore decides to leave the parent group, or (b) the parent group may force the subgroup to leave when the latter challenges the basic group beliefs.

In the first way, in the course of a disagreement, the subgroup members decide that they cannot change group beliefs to their satisfaction and therefore feel that they cannot be part of the parent group. In view of this, the subgroup members often think that they ought to leave their group and establish a new group with different group beliefs. In this case, the subgroup initiates the split and carries it out. An example of this case is the breaking away of a group, later labeled as the Social Democratic Party, from the British Labor Party. This group opposed the leftist platform of the Labor Party, which advocated large-scale nationalization, prohibition by law of nonstate education or medicine, single chamber government, and withdrawal from the Common Market. Because the subgroup was unable to change these beliefs, the subgroup left the party to form a separate political group, the Social Democratic Party (Lindley, 1985).

In the second way, the parent group initiates the split by expelling the subgroup that tries to change group beliefs. In this case, the group members do not agree to change group beliefs and decide that the challenge of the subgroup threatens group unity and efficacy. Therefore, the parent group may cause the split by forcing the subgroup to leave. An illustration of this type of split was provided by Rayner (1986), who analyzed the schisms within the Socialist Worker's Party (previously called International Socialists), a small Trotskyist group in Great Britain. According to the analysis, the party went through ideological changes that consolidated it as a centralized combat organization in the Leninist tradition. In the course of the party's departure from an egalitarian outlook with a democratic framework, a number of groups were forced to leave for not accepting the party's line. Thus, for example, Rayner described the departure of the Revolutionary Opposition (a subgroup in the party) as a result of criticism of the party leader's economic beliefs. After the criticism, the group was forced to part company with the parent organization to form the Worker's League — a new political group.

Once a group splits, the new group will try to differentiate itself from the parental group. The establishment of the new group's own identity is one of its most important tasks. This differentiation is accomplished by emphasizing the uniqueness of the new group and its differences from the parent group. Therefore, special efforts are directed to the formulation and elaboration of the new group beliefs, which demarcate the boundary of the new group and define its special characteristics. The formulated group beliefs have to be noticeably different from the group beliefs of the parent group in order to justify the schism. In the first phase of the formation of the new group, group members make special efforts to disseminate and maintain their group beliefs in order to consolidate their group's existence.

Worchel (1984) proposed a three-stage model of group schism, paying special attention to the establishment of a new identity by the separating group. According to the description, in the first stage — the period of discontent — some of the group members experience dissatisfaction and disenchantment. They feel, on an individual level, that the group does not satisfy their needs. If the group does not address this problem, then the next stage may take place. Two factors may retard the movement to the next stage: (a) an appeal to group loyalty or patriotism, or (b) identification of an outside threat. In the second stage, the discontented group is drawn together, usually following a crisis or a dramatic event. The process of differentiation continues until the group shapes its own identity, which is a characteristic of the third stage. In this stage, the group completes the separation process by drawing clear boundaries, which are reflected in the expression of extreme and uncompromising positions in direct opposition to the parent group's beliefs. The new group formulates its own set of group beliefs, and, in order to close its own ranks, it not only confronts the parent group, but it also develops a climate of rigidity, intolerance, and conformity. It is at this time that "the group often adopts a name, symbol, dress code or uniform, and even a language of its own" (p. 14). After the formation of its own identity and increased cohesiveness, the group moves to the last stage, that of moderation. In this stage, the new group may develop openness as well as cooperation with other groups, including the parent group.

While political groups often merge and split, among religious groups the latter process, called schism, is predominant. Most of the analyses of religious schism suggest that it develops through three stages. First, within a denomination differences of opinion arise over group beliefs. Then, the differences escalate into conflict. Finally, the losing side may leave in order to establish a new denomination (e.g., Etzioni, 1975b; Lehman, 1980). Obviously, the dissident members, if they are not expelled and if they still strive to maintain their group membership, must either become secessionists within the tradition by adopting several new subgroup beliefs while still adhering to the basic group beliefs, or remain in the group, continuing to subscribe to group beliefs and simultaneously attempting to change them in institutionalized ways.

Wilson (1971), analyzing schism within religious groups, suggested that the departing group usually has a disagreement with the parent group over group beliefs pertaining to norms. The allegation often concerns the claim that the parent group departed from the originally formulated group beliefs. In the three analyzed cases, the Protestant Methodist Church left Methodism in 1828 in its attempt to restore the pristine principles of Wesleyanism; the Hicksites separated from Quakers in 1827 because the Hicksites wanted an egalitarian structure in the church; and the Brethren split into Open and Exclusive over the issue of Christ's suffering and the question of open communion. More recently, a schism has taken place in the Protestant Episcopal Church in the U.S.A. (PECUSA) following the decisions to ordain women as priests and to rewrite the 1928 Book of Common Prayer. Thousands of Episcopalians have disagreed with these decisions, which they claim violate the basic group beliefs, and so they have left the church.

Hostetler (1968), analyzing the case of the Amish split from the Swiss Anabaptist movement, elaborated on more phases in the development of sectarian groups. Applying these phases to the present conception of group beliefs suggests that the split takes place in the following process: (a) new beliefs, different from the parent's group beliefs, are formed; (b) a leader with authority promotes the new beliefs and organizes his followers; (c) the leader imposes sanctions on opposing persons or groups; (d) additional specific beliefs are added to make the subgroup unique; and (e) the new group is formed and the new group beliefs differentiate the group from the parent group.

In the case of the Amish split from the Swiss Anabaptist movement, the former group challenged the main movement on three issues: the avoidance of the excommunicated members (Meidung), the excommunication of a woman who had admitted speaking a falsehood, and the belief that the sympathizers of Anabaptists who do not join the group would be saved (Treuherzigen) (Hostetler, 1968). For all these issues, the Amish group, under the leadership of Jakob Ammann, formed its own subgroup beliefs, which preached avoidance of the excommunicated member, excommunication of the lying woman, and rejection of the belief that the sympathizers can be saved. As the subgroup beliefs were formulated, Jakob Ammann polarized the group by demanding a clear decision from Anabaptist communities on these three issues. With time, the subgroup began to differentiate itself even more as new beliefs were added. The subgroup began to have communion service twice a year instead of once a year. The subgroup members began to practice footwashing, to dress uniformly, and to cease to trim their beards. As the pressure by Jakob Ammann to accept the subgroups' beliefs increased, the split was inevitable. Finally, the subgroup parted and established its own separate entity, which, in this stage, expressed much animosity toward the parent group.

All the described models of splits contain similar elements, but differ in the emphases and details they describe. Nevertheless, it is obvious that they all focus on the disagreement about group beliefs as a main cause for the split.

A number of conditions that may determine whether a split will take place have been suggested (Turner & Killian, 1957; Wilson, 1971):

1. a schism is less likely when the dissenting subgroup is well integrated into the parent group;
2. a schism is less likely if the parent group has the power to suppress dissension;
3. a schism is less likely when the parent group has the ability to absorb the dissenting group, either by changing group beliefs or accommodating variability;
4. a schism is more likely in a group in which subgrouping easily takes place;
5. a schism is more likely in groups that are either highly centralized or decentralized, the former because nondecision-making powers are invested in the lower group members and the latter because there is diffusion of coordination and integration;
6. a schism is less likely in groups in which group beliefs pertain to the importance of the group's existence;
7. a schism is less likely in groups with charismatic leaders;
8. a schism is more likely in groups characterized by either extreme dogmatism or extreme openness;
9. a schism is more likely in groups that do not have institutionalized mechanisms to resolve internal conflict; and
10. a schism is more likely in groups that do not provide channels for expressing grievances.

Disintegration

Groups not only merge or split, but also sometimes cease to exist. Although the latter process occurs for many reasons, the present conception focuses on one reason, namely, group beliefs' decadence. In the present view, *disintegration takes place either when group members lose their confidence in group beliefs or when group beliefs become so peripheral in the group members' repertoire that they are almost never accessible.*

The first process may take place when group members receive information that contradicts group beliefs and is successfully established as valid. In this case, the verified, contradictory information causes the validity of group beliefs to decrease. If new beliefs are not substituted for the invalidated beliefs, then the group loses its main basis for identity and, therefore, disintegrates. An example of this situation is the previously described case of the Clamshell Alliance and the Direct Action Task Force, which both disintegrated (Downey, 1986). Both groups carried out unsuccessful activities because they did not succeed in substituting the old group beliefs with new ones. Disagreements over group beliefs and failures paralyzed activity and group members lost interest in their respective groups.

The latter cognitive process occurs when group beliefs cease to be relevant for group members. Implicitly, then, such group beliefs do not satisfy their needs anymore and therefore lose their importance (Zald & Ash, 1965). This process is stimulated by changing conditions in the environment and/or by changing needs of group members. In both cases, static group beliefs, which are not adapted to natural changes, lose their relevance and the process of disintegration begins. The case of the disintegration of the Townsend organization is an example of this situation (Messinger, 1955). The Townsend National Recovery Plan Organization was established in the early 1930s with the goal of "bringing about full industrial production for the Nation . . . and make jobs for jobless." During the Depression, its group beliefs advocated a specific plan of linking pensions to economic reconstruction. However, following World War II, the national membership of the organization declined about 97% from about 2.2 million members in 1936. The main reason for the decline was the irrelevance of group beliefs in new postwar economic conditions. As a result, group members lost interest in group beliefs and the group disintegrated.

Loss of group beliefs is the loss of group identity. It indicates that the group's boundaries cease to exist, and the group is not differentiated from out-groups. In this situation, group members lose interest in group activities and the group's cohesiveness decreases. Gradually, the membership declines and, finally, the group disintegrates.

Summary

Multiple membership in groups is one of the salient characteristics of the human beings. Individuals form groups and spend almost all their lives participating in their activities. In the course of individuals' participation, the groups continuously change as group members themselves persistently form new ideas, modify old ones, and constantly react to and act upon their environment.

There are many different ways to look upon the formation of groups and the transformations they go through. The present conception suggests looking at the cognitive products of group members as a framework for understanding group organization and change. Group members form group beliefs that serve as a uniting bond for their existence. Subsequently, these beliefs function as a prism through which it is possible to comprehend various dynamics of group changes.

Groups merge, form subgroups within their framework, change their essence, split, and disintegrate. In all these processes group beliefs play an important role. In many cases, the focus of these dynamics revolves around group beliefs. Groups, for example, can merge only when their group beliefs are similar. Also, groups split when group members strongly disagree about their group beliefs, and groups disintegrate when group members lose their interest in group beliefs. It is the analysis of group beliefs and their evolvement that sheds a particular light on the changes that take place in groups.

Chapter 7

Case One: German Delegitimizing Beliefs About Jews — 1933–1945

This chapter analyzes a particular example of group beliefs: Germans' delegitimizing beliefs about Jews from 1933 to 1945. There is no doubt that the analysis of a nation's group beliefs is a presumptuous task. An analysis of small-group group beliefs is much easier to perform. But this is precisely the reason I decided to illustrate group beliefs within a societal framework. A convincing case of group beliefs in a large group can be more easily generalized to small groups. Nations, like small groups, have group beliefs, which, as will be described, define their identity and affect their behavior. Specifically, I would like to propose that during the Nazi regime delegitimizing beliefs were widely shared by Germans and defined their "groupness," that is, these beliefs served as group beliefs. In presenting this case, this chapter will first define the concept of delegitimization.

Delegitimization

As indicated, one category of group beliefs may consist of specific negative beliefs that one group may have about another group. In particular, I am referring to beliefs of delegitimization, that is, *beliefs that downgrade another group with extreme negative social categories for the purpose of excluding it from human groups that are considered as acting within the limits of acceptable norms and/or values* (Bar-Tal, D., 1989c). In other words, these group beliefs deny the humanity of the delegitimized group. Dehumanization, outcasting, negative trait characterization, use of political labels, and group comparison are among the most commonly used contents of delegitimization (see, for example, Bar-Tal, D., 1988). Dehumanization involves categorizing a group as inhuman either by using categories of subhuman creatures such as inferior races and animals, or by using categories of negatively valued superhuman creatures such as demons, monsters, and satans. Trait characterization is done by using traits that are evaluated as extremely negative and unacceptable to a given society. The use of labels such as aggressors, idiots, or parasites exemplifies this type of delegitimization. Outcasting consists of categorization into groups that are considered to be violators of pivotal social norms. Outcasting may include such categories as murderers, thieves, psychopaths, or maniacs. The society usually excludes these violators from its system and often places them in total institutions, such as prisons or psychiatric hospitals.

The use of political labels involves categorization into political groups that are considered to be totally unacceptable by the members of the delegitimizing society, as for example, Nazis, fascists, communists, or imperialists. These groups often threaten the basic values of the given society and are considered a danger to its system. Delegitimization by *group comparison* consists of labeling the delegitimized group with the name of another group that serves as an example of negativity in the given society. The use of such categories as "Vandals" or "Huns" is an example of this type of delegitimization. Each society has in its cultural repertoire examples of other groups or societies that serve as symbols of malice, evil, or wickedness.

The definition and the methods of delegitimization not only imply the use of extremely negative and unique contents, the rejection of the delegitimized group to the point of denying its humanity, and the accompanying intensely negative emotions, but also behavioral intentions. Since the contents of delegitimization imply negative behavior that the delegitimized group performs or can potentially enact, the delegitimizing group often feels compelled to take extreme actions in order to avert danger. Thus, delegitimization is often related to negative behavior that the delegitimizing group performs toward the other group (see Bar-Tal, D., in press-b).

The contents of the delegitimizing beliefs may be shared by group members and considered to be one of the characterizations of their groupness. In this case, the delegitimizing beliefs become group beliefs. The most salient example of the above case is the delegitimizing beliefs about Jews held by many Germans during the Nazi regime. The Nazis placed delegitimizing beliefs about Jews at the very core of their ideology (Gordon, 1984; Mosse, 1964; Wistrich, 1985), and the Nazis' ascendence to power enabled them to turn these delegitimization beliefs into group beliefs. In fact, accepting Nazi ideology or even merely supporting the Nazi regime meant, in reality, at least partially adopting their views about Jews, because every aspect of life in Germany between 1933 and 1945 was stamped by these beliefs. That is, these delegitimizing beliefs were not only part of the German dominant ideology, but also became part of the formal laws, folkways, morals, and Gemeinschaft. Thus, the behavior of every ordinary citizen in Germany, in many life domains, was a direct derivative of the delegitimizing beliefs about Jews.

As Dawidowicz (1975) noted:

> Anti-Semitism was the core of Hitler's system of beliefs and the central motivation for his policies. He believed himself to be the savior who would bring redemption to the German people through the annihilation of the Jews, that people who embodied, in his eyes, the Satanic hosts. . . . Generations of anti-Semitism had prepared to accept Hitler as their redeemer. Layer upon layer of anti-Semitism of all kinds— Christian church teachings about the Jews, Volkist anti-Semitism, doctrines of racial superiority, economic theories about the role of Jews in capitalism and commerce, and a half-century of political anti-Semitism—were joined with the solder of German nationalism, providing the structural foundation upon which Hitler and the National Socialist movement built. (pp. 163–164)

A Process of Delegitimizing Jews — 1933–1945

A short historical description may illuminate the process of the delegitimization of Jews in Germany between 1933 and 1945 (see, for example, Noakes & Pridham, 1984). Hitler was appointed Reich Chancellor in January, 1933, and there was an immediate translation of the delegitimizing beliefs into spontaneous outbreaks of anti-Jewish acts all over Germany (see Schleunes, 1966). Jews were attacked in the streets, Jewish businesses were stricken, and Jewish professionals (teachers, lawyers, professors, judges, and doctors) were denounced. This outbreak was followed by an organized boycott of Jews by Germans.

On April 7, 1933, came the inception of anti-Jewish legislation designed to turn Jews into second-class citizens and to hurt them physically. The first set of laws ("Laws for the Restoration of the Professional Civil Service") regulated the Civil Service of public and semipublic bodies, which included all state, provincial, and municipal officials. The laws referred to teachers in schools, professors in universities, doctors and employees in state hospitals, judges, mayors, postmasters, and so on. All employees in these sectors had to produce evidence of the religion of their parents and grandparents to prove their Aryan status. If they could not prove this, then they were to be retired. At first they were to be allowed a small pension, and any German who was of Jewish origin, related to a Jew who had served in the First World War, who had lost a father or son in this war, or who had been an official before the First World War was allowed to retain his post. However, new laws issued in May and June of 1933 made most of the previous exemptions meaningless.

In 1935, Jews were excluded from the army and their names were expunged from the war memorials of the First World War. Then, they were gradually excluded from practicing law and medicine, from cultural and entertainment enterprises, from journalism, and from inheriting farm properties. In addition, Jews were prevented from going into cinemas, theaters, swimming pools, or resorts.

In September, 1935, two laws were introduced at the Nuremberg Rally. One stated that "only a German subject of German or related blood who proves by his attitude that he is willing and fit to serve faithfully the German nation and Reich is a citizen. . . . Only a citizen is vested with full political rights." The second law dealt with the "protection of German blood and honor," and forbade all marriages between Aryans and non-Aryans and all service of Aryan domestics below the age of 45 in a non-Aryan household. Other laws enacted in this period institutionalized Jews' inferior status in every aspect of their lives.

At the same time, the authorities and Germans at large attempted systematically to hurt Jews in commerce and industry via boycotts, regulations, and physical violence. On "Crystal Night" of November 9–10, 1938, Jews were beaten (about 100 were killed), synagogues were burned, and Jewish shops were looted all over the Reich. Following this pogrom, Jews were obliged to pay fines, their movement was restricted, and their children were excluded from German schools.

Beginning January 1, 1939, all Jews were required to carry the middle name Israel or Sarah. In a speech to the German Reichstag of January 30, 1939, Hitler prophesied "the annihilation of the Jewish race in Europe" in the event of war. On

September 1, Germany attacked Poland and the Second World War began. From this date until the surrender of Nazi Germany on May 9, 1945, the Germans carried out an implication of their extreme delegitimizing beliefs—the extermination of European Jewry. This was a genocide on an unprecedented scale, which was performed in a systematic, well-organized, and brutal way (see Staub, 1989). Within 6 years, about 6 million Jews perished as a consequence of mass executions, systematic gassing, deadly epidemics, and starvation.

This description illustrates how the delegitimizing beliefs, adopted as group beliefs, were allowed in a relatively short time to perform what is called today a Holocaust of the Jews (see also Mosse, 1978). Delegitimizing beliefs led to exclusion, social isolation, expropriation and exploitation, expulsions and pogroms, and ultimately, to genocide. Although it should be noted that the delegitimizing beliefs were only one determinant of German behavior, they established the foundation for the political mechanisms to facilitate the described actions. Delegitimizing beliefs are a necessary, but insufficient, condition for such extreme behavior. Moreover, the nature of extremely negative behavior is determined by the content of group beliefs. When the beliefs imply threat, as in the case of the Jews' delegitimization in Nazi Germany, then an attempt to eliminate the delegitimized group may take place.

Contents of German Delegitimizing Beliefs About Jews

The basic content of the delegitimizing beliefs about Jews pertained to their evil, criminality, and inferiority. The Nazis expressed this idea in a wide scope of contents. A partial list of delegitimizing beliefs includes such contents as: Jews are "satanic"; Jews are the "incarnation of destructive drive"; Jews "enslaved German people"; Jews are "devils," "ferment of decomposition," "destroyers of civilization," "world's enemy," "parasites," "sons of chaos," "demons," "bolsheviks," "bacteria, vermin and pests," "degeneration of mankind," "hereditary criminals," "responsible for German misfortune," "oppressors," "inspirers and originators of dreadful catastrophies," "arrogant and aggressive," "international maggots and bedbugs," and Jews "cultivate cholera germs" and "misuse German hospitality."

This list indicates that Jews were delegitimized in all possible ways. They were dehumanized because they were considered to be members of a lower race; at the same time, they were labeled as demons or satans, which are superhuman creatures. They were portrayed as soulless, usurious, sneaky, shallow, insincere, shrewd, materialistic, or rootless. They were outcast because they were also labeled as thieves, corrupters, exploiters, or immoral men.

In addition, Jews were presented with political labels, since they were viewed as promoters of such diverse evils as bolshevism, capitalism, democracy, and internationalism—all aimed at subverting "Aryan racial superiority." By using political labels, Nazi propaganda accused Jews of starting World War I, causing Germany's war defeat, overthrowing the monarchy, directing the revolution, dominating the "Weimar system," precipitating the Great Depression, and polluting the Aryan race. In view of these descriptions, it is not surprising that Jews became symbols of an evil entity and their name was used to delegitimize other groups. Thus, the leaders of the Soviet Union were labeled "Jewish," bolshevism was treated as synonymous with Jewishness, and hostile foreign leaders were also described as Jews. In sum, Jews were presented as threatening the basic values of Aryan culture, and as satanic and hostile forces ready to destroy and pollute all that the Germans held sacred.

German Delegitimizing Beliefs as Group Beliefs

Some of the belief contents just described were held by some Germans prior to 1933. However, with the Nazis' ascendance to power, there was a dramatic increase in the extremity and the scope of anti-Semitic contents. Moreover, during the Nazi regime, they were widely available and were used to redefine the uniqueness of the German people. As Mosse (1964) pointed out, "although anti-Semitism had flourished for more than fifty years, Hitler transformed it into a political vehicle, and the soundness of his move was attested by its favorable reception by the public" (p. 294).

It is possible that Germans "were drawn to anti-Semitism because they were drawn to Nazism, not the other way around" (Allen, 1965, p. 7). However, once they accepted Nazism, the delegitimizing beliefs, as an essential part of Nazism, were absorbed. It is beyond the scope of the present work to determine the exact scope of acceptance of the delegitimizing beliefs by Germans. However, historians widely agree that with the support for the Nazi regime came an acceptance of the anti-Semitic beliefs (e.g. Bauer, 1982; Gordon, 1984; Kershaw, 1985; Mosse, 1964; Steinert, 1977). These delegitimizing beliefs, which satisfied various needs of the group as well as those of individuals (see Bar-Tal, D., in 1989c), were acquired by all the segments of the German society, widely spread, and institutionalized. As Kershaw noted:

> The obsession with the "Jewish Question" chiefly belonged to the Nazi bloc within the "power cartel" of the Third Reich. However, the other power elites showed no hesitation in helping to implement anti-Jewish measures and to turn ideological obsession into policy decisions. (p. 58)

In a short time, they became a distinct and significant part of the German mass repertoire (Hamilton, 1982; Mosse, 1964; Steinert, 1977). Moreover, the delegitimizing beliefs about Jews set the parameters for the normative behavior during a 12-year period. That is, they implied a whole system of behavior, which was practiced by Germans. An interesting analysis by Gordon (1984) points to the gradual increase in the acceptance of the behavioral implications deriving from the delegitimizing beliefs by Germans. It indicates that in the early years of the Nazi regime the public merely supported restrictions on Jews' employment, education, and business, but did not support violent acts. In later years, evidence shows that Germans supported deportation and physical attack. According to Gordon's analysis, the delegitimizing beliefs were fully accepted by the Germans, although they probably objected to complete extermination. That is, in principle, Germans accepted the core of the delegitimizing beliefs that indicated that Jews are an inferior, threatening race and therefore should be treated as second-class citizens who should be isolated and expelled.

Of special interest for the present analysis is the Nazis' success in turning their fundamental anti-Semitic beliefs into an important part of the definition of German "groupness." The delegitimizing beliefs about Jews served as a basis for the definition of who is a German and who is not. Not only did these beliefs formally define the boundaries of the German people in accordance with the racist ideology, but the Nazis also made special efforts to retain the Germans' racial view (Mosse, 1978). It was important for them that individuals adopt anti-Semitism as the new social, political, economic, religious, and intellectual German norm. These beliefs became an important part of German identity. During the Nazi era, these and other beliefs defined the essence of the German people. The Nazis insisted on the addition of the delegitimizing beliefs about Jews to the national ethos. A person who did not subscribe to these beliefs could not be considered as German. A person who openly rejected these beliefs was forced to be outside the realm of social acceptability (Gordon, 1984).

Anti-Semitism in Nazi Germany is one of the few cases in modern times in which delegitimization was legally enforced. Individuals who violated the delegitimizing laws were arrested, persecuted, and even executed. Those who aided Jews were classified as Judenfreunde (friends of Jews) and those who had sexual relations with Jews as Rassenschänder (desecrator of race). Both labels were aimed at delegitimizing those who break the delegitimization laws against Jews (Gordon, 1984). The implantation of the delegitimization beliefs about Jews was a great success. Almost all of the Germans complied with the laws. Millions of Germans took part in implementing and executing the behavioral implications of the delegitimizing beliefs. Virtually all branches of the civil service, economic establishment, cultural institutions, and military system were involved in carrying out anti-Jewish policies.

The Cultural Background of Delegitimization

The formal delegitimization of Jews did not appear on a virgin soil. German anti-Semitism has long roots in German history (Dawidowitz, 1975; Mosse, 1964, 1970; Pulzer, 1964). The Nazis capitalized on centuries of covert hostility, jealousy, and mistrust in order to turn their delegitimization of Jews into group beliefs. A pervading current of hatred, contempt, and rejection of Jews was revealed in almost every aspect of German culture.

During the decades preceding the Nazi regime, anti-Semitism subsisted in various social segments of German society. Years before Nazi ideology became the formal ethos of German people, anti-Semitism was a respected position among intellectuals, as well as by the middle class sector (Bernstein, 1973; Glaser, 1964; Gordon, 1984; Mosse, 1964, 1970, 1978). A salient example of an intellectual basis for anti-Semitism can be found in the Völkish school which, in addition to including such elements as antibourgeois values, nature worship, and romantic and cultural nationalism, propagated seeds of anti-Semitic feelings among Germans (Mosse, 1964, 1970). Völkish thinkers not only perpetuated negative stereotypes of Jews, but also revived old anti-Semitic myths about "Jewish world conspiracy" and used destructive accusations of Jewish predominance in financing and in supporting capitalism, socialism, communism, and internationalism.

This anti-Semitism was based on sophisticated and intellectual arguments derived from (a) Social Darwinism, which legitimized the beliefs in "inferior" and "superior" species; (b) nationalism, which advocated national homogeneity and German purity; and (c) Social Conservatism, which strived to bring back Germany to the "good old days" with good German values uncorrupted by Jews who spread alien ideas (Glaser, 1964; Mosse, 1964; Wistrich, 1985).

In the German political system, there were parties whose platforms openly included anti-Semitic demands. Although these were small groups, they did succeed occasionally in installing their ideas in various social organizations and right wing parties and maintaining them in public. During the pre-Nazi era, the German society was also plagued by numerous anti-Semitic associations and societies, as well as by anti-Semitic publications (books and periodicals), which consistently and continuously promoted anti-Semitic beliefs.

A very important basis for the delegitimization of the Jews was the emergence of racist ideology asserting Aryan superiority over other races, but especially over Jews (Mosse, 1964; Pulzer, 1964). The major proponent of racist ideology was Hans F.K. Gunther, who suggested that racial type represents a person's inner dispositions, such as personality traits or drives. In his books, *The Knight, Death and the Devil* (published in 1921), *Racial Science of the German People* (published in 1922), and *Racial Science of the Jewish People* (published in 1930), he presented the doctrine of Aryan supremacy. Gunther's views propagated the idea that Jews are an inferior race: a mixture of non-European races (Rassengemisch), mostly oriental or inner-Asiatic. He categorized Aryans as being racially superior. They were the most pure, creative, honest, and beautiful.

The delegitimizing beliefs of the Nazis were not presented to a population unfamiliar and/or alien to these ideas, but rather to people who had adopted anti-Semitic beliefs in the past, irrespective of Nazi ideology. It was during the Nazi era that anti-Semitic beliefs became fundamental to the German society. During this period, delegitimizing beliefs about Jews were systematically, continuously, intensively, and extensively presented to the German people. All parts of German society and all of the elements of German culture were utilized to propagate the delegitimizing beliefs about Jews.

Spreading the Delegitimizing Beliefs

During the Third Reich, anti-Semitic beliefs became part of the almost daily diet of the German people. Press, pictures, films, lectures, novels, radio programs, and political speeches continuously and repeatedly expressed these beliefs (see, for example, Mosse, 1966). Nazi propaganda was entirely preoccupied with spreading anti-Semitic beliefs. In the totalitarian Nazi regime all means were used to achieve the end of delegitimizing Jews.

Special effort was directed to the use of the printed word. The editors of every printed outlet was instructed to raise racial issues, including attacks on the historically detrimental role of Jews in Germany and the world, their crimes against the public, or their evil character (Bramsted, 1965; Gordon, 1984; Zeman, 1964). Within this general drive, special attention was given to two books: Hitler's *Mein Kampf*, in which he summarized his ideas, and *Protocols of the Elders of Zion*, one of the most vicious anti-Semitic books. Hundreds of thousands of copies of both books were printed and considered as required literature during the Nazi regime.

In *Mein Kampf*, Hitler expounded on race as the central principle of human existence and explicated the relationship between the Aryans and the Jews. According to Hitler, the resurrection of Germany would never be achieved "without the knowledge of the racial problem and hence of the Jewish problem." In his view, the basic conflict is racial rather than political, economic, or societal. It is an apocalyptic conflict between the Aryans and the Jews, between good and evil.

This framework was even an underlying factor in Hitler's definition of the worker. In principle, the worker was anybody who was of Aryan blood and who toiled with his brain or his hand to make an honest living. The natural enemy of the worker was the Jew, who was thought to live unproductively by exploiting honest German folk. In this vein, Hitler described how Jews pursue world domination and how, through capitalism, liberalism, democracy, and bolshevism, they try to change the social order in order to control the masses. The Aryan race, bearer of human culture and civilization, was chosen to rule the world, but first it had to get rid of Jews, who personify evil and the Devil.

To demonstrate Hitler's extreme anti-Jewish beliefs, Jackel (1981) provided a partial list of expressions that Hitler used in his book to describe the Jews:

> "The Jew is a maggot in a rotting corpse"; "he is a plague worse than the Black Death of former times"; "a germ-carrier of the worst sort"; "mankind's eternal germ of disunion"; "the drone which insinuates its way into the rest of mankind"; "the spider that slowly sucks the people's blood at its pores" . . . . (p. 58)

Protocols of the Elders of Zion was also given a prominent place in the effort to spread the delegitimizing beliefs about Jews. This book claimed to provide the evidence for the Jewish plot to control the world. It was originally forged by the czarist secret police at the turn of this century, and its contents describe meetings of Jewish leaders in which they contemplate their secret plans of conspiracy. The book first appeared in German in 1920, and, during the Nazi regime, it received a prominent place. On its basis, innumerable articles and pamphlets were written and later distributed.

Spreading the delegitimizing beliefs about Jews was accomplished not only directly through ideological books or propaganda pamphlets, but also through literary works and daily newspapers. For example, *Eher*, the official Nazi publishing house, issued novels in which a description of Jewish cruelty was the central theme. Also, the press was directed to present the delegitimizing beliefs. Specific anti-

Semitic materials that appeared in speeches, publications, or films were recommended. Moreover, specific terminology was dictated in order to describe the issue. Thus, for example, the emphasis was on "criminality" and the "conspiracy" of Jews against Germany (Gordon, 1984). Of special distinction toward achievement of this goal was the journal *Der Stürmer*, which, under the editorship of Julius Streicher, presented the most vicious attacks on Jews in its articles, pictures and caricatures. The journal, which appealed to sexual-sadistic instincts, helped to spread anti-Semitism among Germans and to establish a general atmosphere of intimidation.

Even children were not spared from direct propaganda aimed at delegitimizing Jews. German children and adolescents were taught to hate and despise Jews. Many school books contained anti-Semitic contents and pictures which depicted the Jews as evil. Also, the teachers were directed to devote special lessons to discuss the Jewish question. Out of school, much of the children's literature focused on anti-Semitic stories. For example, *Der Stümer* published a picture book in which the devil was presented as the father of the Jews and continued with frightening illustrations portraying Jews in satanic ways, and as polluters of German blood and life.

The intellectual sector, including the universities, also took part in this anti-Semitic, orchestrated "festival." In some universities efforts were devoted to substantiating, confirming and extending the beliefs of delegitimization about Jews. University professors like Hans Günther, Johann von Leers, and Siegfried Passarge specialized in the study of the Jewish race and the differences between Jews and Aryans. Their studies provided "scientific" justification for the Nazi doctrine. For example, Johann von Leers, who was a full professor at the University of Jena, specialized in the *Protocols* and other tales. In the foreword to his 1942 book, *The Criminal Nature of the Jews*, he wrote:

> If the hereditary criminal nature of Jewry can be demonstrated, then not only is each people morally justified in exterminating the hereditary criminals—but any people that still keeps and protects Jews is just as guilty of an offense against public safety as someone who cultivates cholera germs without observing the proper precautions.

Nazis even used art in their attempt to control people's beliefs and to spread anti-Semitism, removing the distinction between art and propaganda (Milton, 1980). Racial anti-Semitism was a theme which Nazis thought was important to emphasize in German art. On the one hand, they encouraged a focus on the beauty and nobility of the Aryans, while, on the other hand, they emphasized the ugliness and repulsiveness of the Jews. For example, in November 1939 a Munich exhibit entitled "Wandering Jew" was aimed at showing the history of Jews in a delegitimizing way.

The German film industry produced a number of tracts in which the delegitimizing beliefs of Jews were the major themes. *Die Rothschilds, Jud Süss*, and *Der Ewige Jude* are three notable examples of anti-Semitic films (Richards, 1973). In all of the delegitimizing films, Jews were stereotyped in their physiognomy, their manner of talking, their clothing, and their body structures. They looked greasy, fat, hook-nosed, black-haired, and wore traditional Jewish clothes. More importantly, these films portrayed Jews as physically repellent, extremely greedy and sneaky, driven by sexual urges, exploiting Germans, performing evil deeds, and exhibiting sinister and satanic behavior. The films highlight the fundamental difference between Jews and Germans—between the good, noble, pure Aryans and evil, rotten, and shrewd Jews. In the most focused documentary about Jews, *Der ewige Jude (The Eternal Jew)*, the narrator says:

> Jews have no indigenous civilization; they are unclean; they are not poor, they simply prefer to live in a state of squalor; their community life is on the streets; they hardly ever make anything for themselves; they do not want to work. Their only desire is to trade; their pride lies in haggling over a price. They have no ideals; their divine law teaches them to be selfish, to cheat any non-Jew. (Richards, 1973, p. 345)

Functions of Delegitimizing Beliefs

The delegitimizing beliefs about Jews served several functions, such as enhancing feelings of superiority, increasing group uniformity, and scapegoating. With regard to the first function, groups come in contact and/or have relations with other groups. In these cases, one group usually tries to achieve superiority over another group. These attempts reflect a need that characterizes a group—a need to feel superior in comparison to other groups. Groups compete with each other and, through comparison, strive to feel better, more successful, victorious, more developed, or more moral and humane. Delegitimization enables them to feel superior in comparison to the delegitimized group. It lowers the evaluation of the other group, indicating that the inferior group possesses very negative characteristics and should be excluded from the commonly accepted groups. The use of a delegitimizing category implies that the other group is rejected, since it does not stand in accordance with the norms or values of the delegitimizing group. It denies humanity to the delegitimized group. Labels such as thieves, untrustworthy people, parasites, inferiors, or exploiters discriminate and sharpen the difference between the delegitimizing and the delegitimized groups. They stigmatize the members of the latter group. In this way, delegitimization enables members to feel superiority over the delegitimized group by boasting the sense of their own identity in comparison to the other group.

As Hartmann (1984) expressed it:

> Anti-Semitism not only allowed for extreme forms of scapegoating, but also it is linked to what may well be the most enticing feature of Nazism: the delusion of German superiority. The indifference and the unemotional quality of contempt signify narcissistic grandiosity no less than does vengeful rage. The emotional appeal of Nazism focused on images of greatness, purity, and impregnability. Beyond economic despair and political troubles, Nazism answered to forceful emotional needs. It offered opportunity to distance oneself from the weak, the vulnerable, and the ugly. (p. 639)

Each group strives to maintain its uniformity, which is one of the bases for a group's existence. Members of an enduring group are likely to display at least some central beliefs of striking homogeneity. Lack of group uniformity may cause a low level of cohesiveness in a group and may even result in its disintegration. To avoid such processes, a group often applies pressures on their members to bring about uniformity of beliefs, attitudes and behaviors. Delegitimization of Jews was one of the primary ways to enforce unity. It allowed "the transformation of the ideology into a 'fighting movement,' for it made the abstract concrete for the purposes of mass suggestion" (Mosse, 1966, p. xxvii). The delegitimizing beliefs about Jews first allowed the Nazi party to unite, and later the German people as a whole (Mosse, 1964). By promoting anti-Semitism the Nazis succeeded in uniting the middle and working classes of Germany. This emphasis provided a legitimate call for German transformation (Mosse, 1964). Once these simple and acceptable beliefs became group beliefs, they defined the boundaries of the German nation. They were the uniting glue that channeled various disagreements, frustrations, and disappointments into an area of wholesale agreement.

The pressure to maintain uniformity is applied especially in situations of threat. It therefore is not surprising that one major objective of delegitimization was to create a symbol of energy and evil (Cohn, 1967). The delegitimizing beliefs about Jews with their demonological content provided the evidence for the possible threat. Accordingly, delegitimization of Jews not only strengthened party unity, but also aimed at the creation of consensus and the isolation of opponents. The threat of Jewry was used as a justification for attack on rival socialists, communists, or churchmen. Groups that opposed Nazi policies were identified as Jewish sympathizers. The Nazi regime applied extremely high pressure to maintain the delegitimizing beliefs, including all means of terror (Allen, 1965; Bracher, 1971). Individuals who opposed the delegitimizing beliefs were punished severely, including punishment by death, while conformists were presented as exemplars of German society.

Moreover, the delegitimization of the Jews not only served as a uniting vehicle and as a justification for an elimination of internal opposition, but also as a justification for a war: Nazis consistently identified Germany's enemies (Britain, the United States, the Soviet Union, or Poland) as being dominated by Jews and, therefore, a threat to Germany. Any criticism of German policy abroad served as evidence for Jewish world conspiracy.

As early as the late 30s, groups of psychologists who explored the link between frustration and aggression connected the frustrations of Germans with the ease with which they adopted overt anti-Semitism (Dollard et al., 1939). Delegitimization of Jews served to displace anger, frustration, or disappointment from an original, often ambiguous target. Later, several historians pointed to the scapegoating functions that the delegitimization of Jews fulfilled (e.g., Glaser, 1964; Gordon, 1984). Glaser noted that

> the Jewish minority in Germany was large enough to serve as the general garbage dump of resentments and as an outlet for uncompensated feelings of inferiority. On the other hand, it was so small and encapsulated that discrimination would not bring about any particular damage to the socio-economic fabric of the people. (p. 220)

Gordon pointed out that scapegoating allowed the Nazi regime "to divert the population from other issues, particularly those vague promises of economic and social change that the Nazis had not fulfilled" (p. 149).

Summary

The above analysis suggests that in Nazi Germany, the delegitimizing beliefs about Jews served as group beliefs for two main reasons. First, they were widely shared by the German population. Second, they were used to define the groupness of German people. They provided a common basis with which Germans could identify and through which they defined the boundaries of their own group. All of the institutions of the German society formally adopted and practiced delegitimizing beliefs about Jews. These group beliefs were the most common and useful weapons of Nazi propaganda as a revolutionary catalyst. From Nazi ideology, Germans grew to accept the deep-rooted beliefs that Jews were responsible for the alienation of humanity from the natural order and were the main obstacle to human redemption. Therefore, Germans were convinced that it was necessary to exclude Jews from the economic, political, societal, and cultural aspects of life and to deny their humanity.

The success of the Nazis in turning the delegitimizing beliefs about Jews into group beliefs can be explained both by the existing background of anti-Semitism in the German society and later by the widespread acceptance of, approval of, and collaboration with the Nazi dogma (Hartmann, 1984). Concerning the latter explanation, the Nazi dogma significantly helped to shape the reality of the German people because it was absorbed by the overwhelming majority of Germans.

The present approach suggests that adherence to group beliefs insures group endurance and cohesion. It therefore is not surprising that once the delegitimizing beliefs became group beliefs, Nazis exerted special efforts to maintain and strengthen them. Since the anti-Semitic beliefs were the focus of the Nazi dogma, a rejection of these beliefs implied, in actuality, an opposition to Nazi ideology. Thus, while some of the Germans readily compiled and accepted the beliefs, many Germans accepted them because they identified with the führer, or they internalized the beliefs in the process of their socialization and persuasion (Steinert, 1977).

Over time, as the delegitimizing beliefs about Jews became group beliefs, Germans ascribed much validity to them and they became central in the German repertoire. They became part of the German ethos and were formally institutionalized. Indeed, German delegitimizing beliefs about Jews dominated the public repertoire, affecting every aspect of life until May 8, 1945.

Chapter 8

Implications

The proposed conception implies that group beliefs, like all beliefs, exist in the individual's mind. It does not suggest viewing them as a special entity of the "group mind" category, in the sense that they are superindividual. Beliefs are related to individuals. Groups, organizations, societies, or any other collectivities do not hold beliefs on the collective level—only individual members in the aggregate groups do. However, the present conception describes a widely recognized phenomenon: that group members share beliefs and that these beliefs may be viewed as defining the essence of the group as a whole. That is, it suggests that group beliefs are more than a mere sum of group members' personal beliefs. Sharing of beliefs by group members and a recognition that beliefs characterize them provide group beliefs with distinguished properties. These structural properties of a dynamic whole, a group, are different from the structural properties of the comprising parts, the individuals. In this vein, Lewin (1947) pointed out that "There is no more magic behind the fact that groups have properties of their own, which are different from the properties of their subgroups or their individual members, than behind the fact that molecules have properties, which are different from the properties of the atoms or ions of which they are composed" (p. 8). These properties have important implications for group members as individuals and for the group as a whole. These implications will now be discussed.

Group Beliefs and Groups

Group Beliefs as a Foundation for Group Existence

First of all, group beliefs serve as a foundation for group existence. As presented in previous chapters, they provide the common basis with which individuals can identify and through which they can define their membership in the group. All groups have to have group beliefs, and a necessary condition for the emergence of any group is a formation of group beliefs. That is, in order for individuals to feel that they have something in common that distinguishes them from out-groups, they need to have at least one group belief. The fundamental group belief, "We are a group," shared by group members is a basis on which other group beliefs are added. Group beliefs, which characterize the group, demarcate its boundaries with the out-groups. They differentiate between the in-group and out-group members by underlying the uniqueness of the group. Group members acquire group beliefs and hold them in their repertoire.

Group Beliefs as a Basis for Group Members' Reality

Second, group beliefs provide the psychological framework that allows group members to structure their social reality about the group. The structure of social reality is provided on the basis of the information that group beliefs furnish. This reality is held with certainty because group members tend to attribute high confidence to their contents, considering them as facts and verities. Along this line, Turner and Giles (1981) suggested that on the basis of self-categorization as group members, individuals "change the content of the self-concept from individual differences and unique personality traits to shared stereotypes of attitudes, values, goals, norms, etc. associated with social category membership" (p. 27). As a consequence, there is enhancement of perceptual interchangeability among the group members, which, in turn, produces mutual cohesiveness and even relative uniformity.

Also, group beliefs facilitate the symbolic communication within a group. Group members form their own symbols, which often are unique to their group, and they attribute the same meaning to many other symbols. By sharing the symbols that are always underlain by beliefs, they acquire a common understanding, at least on matters related to this group. This is one of the bases of their uniformity and commonality.

In this respect, group beliefs may be viewed as glasses through which group members perceive their group. The more central the group beliefs are in the group members' repertoire and the more complete they are in covering various aspects of group members' lives, the wider are the perspectives of these glasses. In groups in which group beliefs refer to a wide spectrum of contents covering various aspects of an individual's life, they provide almost a total perspective on the world. In other groups, group beliefs may pertain to specific contents and therefore provide a perspective only on a particular issue that serves as the basis for the group's existence. Furthermore, since group beliefs define the essence of the group, group members who consider their membership as an important part of their life tend to organize their personal beliefs accordingly. Group beliefs often provide the frame of reference for other beliefs. In this situation, group members draw implications from group beliefs and form personal beliefs consistent with them.

Group Beliefs as a Basis for Group Structure

Group beliefs have an effect not only on group members' cognitive outcomes, but also on a group's structural characteristics. They may shed light on the traditionally studied elements of group structure, such as group cohesiveness or subgrouping, as discussed in Chapters 5 and 6 of this book.

In reference to cohesiveness, group beliefs can reflect the extent of "groupness" or feelings of togetherness. The degree of the centrality of group beliefs in group members' repertoire, the extent of confidence in them, and the number of central group beliefs that group members hold may serve as an index of "groupness." The more centrally that group beliefs are held in group members' repertoires and the more confidence group members have in them, the more they feel togetherness.

The feeling of "groupness," as reflected in the belief "We are a group" (i.e., how central it is for group members and how much confidence they have in it), may be one indicator of cohesiveness. Indeed, several researchers used this view either by assessing the evaluation of a group as a whole (e.g., Bovard, 1951), or by measuring the closeness and identification with a group (e.g., Indik, 1965). However, in addition to these direct measurements of cohesiveness, it is also possible to assess the extent of group members' acceptance of group beliefs.

Group beliefs also provide a basis for understanding a subgrouping. Many groups contain subgroups that form their own subgroup beliefs, while at the same time accept the basic group beliefs of the group. Analyzing subgroups' beliefs and their reference to group beliefs allows an understanding of some of the causes for the formation and structure of subgroups.

Group Beliefs as an Influence Tool

Group beliefs provide the group members with special power. The mere perception that group members share group beliefs implies a sense of strength. Converse (1964) suggested in his classic analysis of beliefs that the number of people associated with a particular belief system is an important factor in the political arena:

> ... claims to numbers are of some modest continuing importance in democratic systems for the legitimacy they confer upon demands; and much more sporadically, claims to numbers become important in nondemocratic systems as a threat of potential coercion. (p. 207)

In addition, the power of group beliefs is derived from the perception of unity and commonality that may characterize group members who are aware of sharing group beliefs. One consequence of this perception is that group beliefs may serve as a basis for the demands and desires of group members. Leaders of the group usually take into consideration the group's beliefs when they make decisions that affect the group's life. Being aware that group members share a belief, are aware of sharing it, and are influenced by the belief in their behavior, leaders pay special attention to group beliefs.

Group beliefs reflect the direction that group members desire to take in their behavior. Therefore, leaders frequently make decisions regarding the group's course of action that correspond to group beliefs. From the leaders' perspective, group beliefs may be utilized as a justification for their course of action, since, in many cases, group beliefs specify group goals, values, or ideology. Of relevance to this implication is an analysis by Seliktar (1986), who recognizes the contribution of societal belief systems to a better understanding of leaders' actions in the political sphere. She proposed that on the basis of the belief system, decision-makers may select their choices in response to certain contingencies:

> A belief system may be seen as a set or range of discrete rather than deterministic alternatives on which decision-makers can act. Given the constraints imposed by the external and internal environment of the foreign policy system, one cannot infer directly from a collective belief system to a particular decision. Nevertheless, the belief system can serve as a collective "cognitive map" of the foreign policy environment. (p. 329)

Furthermore, group beliefs serve not only as a basis for selection of a course of action, but also as standards against which group members and the leaders can evaluate group progress and adherence to goals.

Group Beliefs and Intergroup Relations

Group beliefs may determine the attitudes and behaviors of an out-group toward the group. Group beliefs provide important information for out-groups about any given group. Out-groups learn about group beliefs through formal presentations as well as through their implicit expressions, such as leaders' speeches. This information serves as an input in decisions taken in relation to that group. They characterize the group and may even imply the behavior that the group may take.

Group beliefs may indicate possible goals, ideology, values, history, norms, or characteristics of the group. This information enables acquaintanceship with the group and, in turn, influences the type of intergroup relations that may develop. Group beliefs may imply a threat to another group or possible cooperation. A contradiction between group beliefs of two groups may lead to conflict and confrontation, whereas similarity of group beliefs may underlie accordance and collaboration.

Group Beliefs as a Determinant of Group Behavior

Finally, if one assumes that group members act consistently with their beliefs, then group beliefs may be considered an important source for understanding group behavior. This assumption was advanced by various social scientists (e.g., Asch, 1952; Axelrod, 1976; Holsti, 1962; Parsons, 1951). Smelser (1963) even defined collective behavior as "*mobilization on the basis of a belief which redefines social action*" (p. 8). He suggested that shared or, as he called them, generalized beliefs, are necessary for collective action.

Krech and Crutchfield (1948) are among the few social psychologists who pointed out the relationship between beliefs and group behavior. According to them, "the double role of beliefs—in shaping action designed to satisfy needs and in creating new tensions which must be released—becomes particularly important in an analysis of group behavior of people" (p. 386).

Similarly, Sherif and Cantril (1947) noted that

> a cardinal fact concerning the behavior of individual members in any collective situation stands out in high relief: the fact that once an individual identifies himself with a group and its collective actions, his behavior is in a major way determined

by the direction of the group action, whatever this direction may be, good or bad, constructive or destructive. (p. 290)

Even in the initial stages of group formation, following individuals' categorization as group members and the development of minimal interdependence, the influence of group beliefs was detected. In these situations it was found that, through their behavior, group members favored their own group and discriminated against the outgroup (Horwitz & Rabbie, 1989). This behavior showed that group members behaved consistently with their belief, indicating that a group was formed, because one of the widely accepted elementary group norms prescribes preference for one's own group by comparison to out-groups (Le Vine & Campbell, 1972).

Group beliefs provide the cognitive basis for many group behaviors. They supply a prescriptive formula—a guide to individual and collective action. Often, they set rules for how to act, specify goals that may be pursued, and indicate the means used to achieve these goals. In addition, group beliefs may offer an explanation, a justification, and legitimacy for the selected direction of behavior. In other words, group beliefs may function as guiding forces for a group and, therefore, may determine the direction, intensity, and persistence of group behavior. This is one of the most important implications of group beliefs. Although it is not claimed that group beliefs can explain group behavior in totality, group beliefs provide a framework which illuminates one of the determinants of group action.

In sum, the presented conception suggests going beyond the traditionally investigated structural group characteristics and processes to examine the cognitive basis and products of a group's entity. In terms of the controversy in the early days of social psychology (see Steiner, 1986) between those psychologists who suggested that groups have a reality quite apart from the particular individuals who participate in them (e.g., McDougall, 1920) and those who suggested that groups are only abstractions from collections of individuals' ideas (e.g., Allport, F., 1924b), the present approach takes the middle road. It neither accepts the proposition that a group feels, thinks, or decides as an entity, or the view that social and collective behavior can be fully explained by "stimulations and reactions arising between an individual and the social portion of his environment; that is between the individual and his fellows" (Allport, F., 1924a, p. 3). Group members, by forming a shared reality and uniform beliefs, constitute a unit that can be characterized by holistic features. Although in this entity, group members feel, think, and act, the meaning of their common action and products can be understood only by taking a holistic perspective.

People live and act in groups. They follow rules of behavior that cannot be described and explained in terms of the properties of the individuals comprising them. Groups have properties of their own that cannot be reduced to those of individuals. The summation of group members' thoughts, feelings, and behaviors cannot exhibit the whole picture. Only a focus on the totality of processes, structures, or outcomes can explain group life.

From this perspective, group beliefs characterize a group. They only have a meaning when individuals in a collective perceive themselves as one entity. Group beliefs, then, describe the basis for group togetherness and influence not only the individuals, but also the structure, processes, and behaviors of the group as a whole.

Group Beliefs and Social Cognition

The proposed conception also has an implication for the study of social cognition. Social psychologists who have studied social cognition have focused mainly on the individual; they have investigated beliefs and attitudes as processed through intrapersonal processes, their structures in the individual's mind, and their effect on the individual's mind, and their effect on the individual's behavior. Simon (1976), summarizing a symposium about cognition and social behavior, noted more than a decade ago that social psychologists dealing with cognition excluded groups, retreating to the "social psychology of one." Not much has been changed since then. So the study of social cognition has continued to be mainly the study of the individual. This line of research overlooks the fact that group members share beliefs and also acquire them through intragroup processes. Social cognition studies, by extending their focus to groups, can widen the perspective on social cognitive processes and products of group members. They can expand *a social* aspect to the study of cognition.

Knowledge is social. Much of any individual's knowledge is acquired from other people and is shared by them. This knowledge depends for its meaning on previously constructed group concepts and beliefs in which the term *experience* is framed. In this respect, the acquired knowledge contributes to group differences (Bar-Tal, D., & Kruglanski, 1988). Moreover, the shared knowledge not only has an impact on individual's behavior, but also underlies many of the intragroup and intergroup processes. Some of these processes are the subject of this book.

Forgas (1981) articulated the present view in the following way:

> Social cognition cannot be reduced to individual cognition. This relates to the notion that ideas, thoughts and representations are processed collectively as well as individually. The way a dyad or a group comes to weigh up, integrate and make sense of information is intrinsically different from the corresponding activities of isolated individuals.
>
> . . . Just as we can talk about uniquely group phenomena in the fields of decision-making, problem solving or categorization, there also exists an even more complex cultural-collective level at which ideas, beliefs, and representations are processed. Perhaps a rather obvious, but often neglected point about such social thought and social representations is that they cannot be explained in terms of individual psychological process. (p. 267)

The present conception shifts the preoccupation with social knowledge from individuals to groups. It provides a framework to analyze social cognitive processes and products in social contexts of groups. This framework strengthens the social perspective of contemporary social psychology. The presented analysis explains uniformity of group members as reflected in their beliefs, which, in turn, influences their behavior in a direction of commonality. This analysis recognizes individual differences of members in the same group, but, at the same time, focuses on collective social reality, a relatively disregarded topic of social psychology. It is this reality that casts social context into the studies of individuals' cognition contents. A similar point was made by Tajfel (1984) who noted that the

> task of social psychology is the study of social situations in which the long-lasting or temporary identifications with some groups, and differentiations from others, bring about a large variety of forms of collective behavior which can range from a carnival organized by an ethnic minority to deep rumblings capable of shaking up a whole social system. (p. 712)

The study of group beliefs concerns not only group processes or structures, but also contents per se. The mapping of group beliefs is a necessary condition for understanding the dynamics of the specific group. The contents indicate the group's goals, values, or norms. They point out the available repertoire of group members. The study of contents may describe what beliefs are central or are held with much confidence (see for example, Bar-Tal, D., 1986, 1988, 1989a, in press-a; Bar-Tal, D., & Antebi, 1989). All these topics shed light on group behavior.

Already over three decades ago, Newcomb (1951) noted that

> most social psychologists of primarily psychological persuasion take no systematic account of the facts of the social environment in which human organisms live. More specifically, they minimize or even ignore the nature of the social structure of which their subjects are members. (p. 32)

Nevertheless, American social psychology has especially developed primarily individualistic orientation (Bar-Tal, D., 1984; Israel & Tajfel, 1972; Pepitone, 1981; Sampson, 1977). Sampson pointed out that "psychology plays an important role in reinforcing an individualistic, self-contained perspective; it helps play down the importance of interdependent values" (p. 780). Pepitone noted that social psychology, by overemphasizing its individuocentric perspective,

> cannot adequately deal with the influences on personality and social behavior that originate in the objective environment, including especially the social structure and normative systems in which individuals are embedded and psychologically subscribed. (p. 983)

This picture may be changing somewhat, especially in view of recent developments in European social psychology. Contributions by Tajfel (1981, 1982, 1984b), Turner (1987), Moscovici (1976), Farr and Moscovici (1984), and Billig (1978) suggest new avenues for studying beliefs and attitudes as group products. These avenues not only introduce social context, but some of them also direct special attention to macro groups.

Individuals not only engage in dyadic relations, or act in small groups, but are also members of political parties, religious denominations, ethnic groups, or nations. This fact cannot be disregarded by social psychologists. Group members' behavior can be studied on various levels and from different perspectives. As a complementary addition to sociological, anthropological, political, or economic contributions, social psychologists may provide unique input to the study of large groups by focusing on their cognitive products, the shared beliefs.

There is a significant difference between situations in which a belief is held as personal and those in which it is held as a group belief. In the first case, personal beliefs may explain the individual's affect and behavior, while, in the latter, group beliefs may shed light on organized and coordinated behavior of group institutions. Taking a specific example, there is a meaningful difference when an individual or individuals hold prejudiced beliefs and when these beliefs are viewed as group beliefs. On the basis of the analyzed case of German delegitimizing beliefs about Jews during the Nazi era, it becomes apparent that group beliefs have special dynamics and consequences. They may guide the selection of group goals, policies, and coordinated action. In contrast, personal beliefs (except when held by a leader) or even common beliefs do not have the same effect and power.

This view is recognized by social scientists who make special efforts to study shared beliefs, or, as they often call it, belief systems (e.g., Almond & Verba, 1965; Geertz, 1973; Parsons, 1951). Mannheim (1952) pointed out that the thoughts of the individuals are underlain by the collective purpose of a group and "in this connection it becomes more clear that a large part of thinking and knowing cannot be correctly understood, as long as its connection with existence or with the social implications of human life are not taken into account" (p. 241).

Conclusions

Group belief conception provides a cognitive and social perspective for the study of a group. The existence of a group is a social reality for group members. Group beliefs provide the basis that allows group members to view the group as a social reality. The group, then, is a product not only of structural characteristics, environment, situational conditions, motivational tendencies, or social influence, but also of personal cognitive processes. These processes determine the essence of the group, since group beliefs provide the contents that serve as bases for group formation and group maintenance.

Beliefs cannot exist independently of individuals or externally to them. Group members as individuals are the ones who cognize the beliefs and turn them into their reality. In this respect, group beliefs do not imply anything mystical or supernatural. Individuals form group beliefs and process them in the same way as personal beliefs. The intrapersonal process described in Chapter 1 is the one that also describes the formation and change of group beliefs on a personal level. However, group beliefs have special meaning different from individuals' beliefs or common beliefs. Since group members are aware of sharing them, they acquire a special quality, unlike when individuals hold personal beliefs, are unaware of sharing them, and do not consider them as characterizing their group.

It is important for social psychologists to study the contents of group beliefs and the process through which group members acquire them, become aware of sharing them, and are affected by them in their behavior. This line of interest, on the one hand, adds a cognitive aspect to the study of a group and, on the other hand, liberates beliefs from their individual closet to extend their social meaning. In this respect, the present approach provides the bridge between the individual's level of analysis and the group's level. Group members, as individuals, are the ones who acquire beliefs that shape their reality. However, when group members become aware of the fact that their beliefs are shared by other group members, these beliefs acquire a special quality. That is, group beliefs may have important cognitive, affective, and even behavioral implications for the group members as individuals and for the group as a whole. At the same time, they may also have influence on the structure of the group, as well as on the various social processes that take place in its framework. Future studies could shed light on these implications.

Postscript

Because the first chapter began with a short description of the nonjustificational approach to the philosophy of science, which served as a guideline for the analysis of group beliefs, the ending of this book will discuss the implications of the presented conception for the development of science. In particular, it will focus on a functioning of scientific groups and changing of their group beliefs. Thus, this postscript closes the full circle that began in the first chapter. That is, although some ideas of the philosophy of science had influence on the present conception, it seems that, in turn, the framework may illuminate several phenomena related to knowledge formation by scientists.

Groups of Scientists

The discussion of the implications is possible because scientists, like other people, organize themselves in groups for various purposes, such as to create ideas, to advance their professional goals, to propagate theories, to define the boundaries of their disciplines, or to strengthen their professional identity (e.g., Blume, 1974; Crane, 1972; Mulkay, 1977). In this vein, Kuhn (1970) observed that it is possible to identify groups of scientists on different levels, beginning with a global community (for example, all natural scientists), continuing through disciplinary communities, to groups that support a specific theory. Such groups of scientists develop shared definitions of their work, paradigms that interpret findings and guide new research. In other words, scientists adjust to the problems of dealing with knowledge in their fields by forming groups of various kinds based upon communication and shared beliefs.

Scientists' associations within the framework of groups can be either formal or informal. In the former case, scientists define group goals, set rules, establish channels of communication, elect governing institutions, organize meetings, and even select group members. Formal groups can be formed to advance science in general (e.g., the American Association for the Advancement of Science), a specific discipline (e.g., the American Psychological Association, the European Association of Experimental Social Psychology, the American Chemical Society), a specific subject area (e.g., the International Society of Political Psychology), or a specific approach or theory (e.g., the Jean Piaget Society, the Jung Foundation for Analytical Psychology).

Informal groups are usually organized around certain ideas—often to support a theory, a conceptual framework, or a paradigm. Although these groups do not have elected governing institutions or formally written goals and rules, group members do establish communication channels, recruit new members, organize meetings, and often crystalize particular identity (e.g., Halmos, 1957; Mullins, 1972; Price & Beaver, 1966). An example of an informal group of scientists is described by Price and Beaver. In this case, the Division of Research Grants of the National Institutes of Health organized a group specializing in Oxidative Phosphorylation and Terminal Electron Transport. The group was established in February 1961 with 32 members and by June 1965 it had grown to 592 members. The group established a system of exchanging information (especially preprints of papers), constructed a means for extending its membership, and formed ways for the group's interaction.

Scientists' Group Beliefs

If we accept the observation that scientists organize themselves in groups, then we can assume that scientific groups, like other groups, have group beliefs. These group beliefs characterize groups of scientists. Their specific contents can be of wide scope, such as defining the nature of a subject area (e.g., a discipline), explaining the limits of the membership (e.g., what is required from a person to be accepted as a group member), describing the content area of interest, designating accepted methodology, or even naming specific theoretical beliefs that a member has to hold. A few examples of possible group beliefs taken from written materials will illustrate some of their contents.

The Jean Piaget Society opens its membership "to anyone interested in the nature of human knowledge, the processes of knowing and their development" (undated flier). This society follows the themes of study of Jean Piaget, who "has exerted seminal influence on all scholars concerned with human knowing and its development. Starting as a biologist interested in the history of scientific thinking, he approached heretofore exclusive philosophical questions in a resolutely empirical fashion and created epistemology as a science, separate from philosophy, but interrelated with all human sciences" (undated flier).

The Psychometric Society is composed of a group of individuals interested in the development of psychology as a quantitative science. The focus of the work of its members is on developing mathematical models and procedures for analyzing psychological data.

The International Society of Political Psychology outlines its objective as

> . . . to facilitate communication across disciplinary, geographic, and political boundaries among scholars and concerned individuals in government and public posts, the communications media, and elsewhere who have a scientific interest in the relationship between political and psychological processes. . . . To increase the quality, breadth, depth and usefulness of work in political psychology. (undated brochure)

Of relevance to the conception of group beliefs held by scientists in Kuhn's (1970) discussion about the shared beliefs of scientific communities. He pointed out that groups of scientists share

> disciplinary matrix—"disciplinary" because it refers to the common possession of the practitioners of a particular discipline; "matrix" because it is composed of ordered elements of various sorts, each requiring further specification. (p. 182)

Kuhn identified four types of shared disciplinary matrix: (a) "symbolic generalizations," which refer to formalized rules; (b) "metaphysical paradigms," which refer to beliefs in particular models and heuristics; (c) "values," which provide criteria for prediction, judgments of theory, etc.; and (d) "exemplars," which are concrete problem solutions presented in the discipline.

On the basis of the conception presented in the previous chapters, it is possible to propose that group beliefs demarcate the boundary for groups of scientists. They indicate who is a group member and they differentiate various groups within the scientific community. They define the raison d'être for the group existence and describe its essence. In this respect, they establish the identity of scientists' groups. On their basis it is possible to know a group's unique characteristics. In other words, group beliefs provide the credo or dogma for a group of scientists. Usually, they delineate the principles in which scientists believe and refer to basic premises that unite them in their work. Accordingly, the contents of group beliefs outline the framework that underlies the scientific endeavor of the particular group.

Furthermore, it can be assumed that an advance of meaningful scientific ideas requires turning them into group beliefs. Such development implies that the ideas have followers who accept them, consider them as important, interact on their basis, and try to disseminate them. Ideas around which groups are not formed may disappear. Similarly, when a group organized around ideas, which serve as group beliefs, disintegrates or dissolves, these ideas may move into oblivion. The history of Invariant Theory in mathematics, as described by Fisher (1967), corresponds to the latter case. With time, for various reasons, the group of Invariant Theorists did not have a continuation and therefore "Invariant Theory is indeed dead" (p. 243).

Whereas the fundamental group belief ("We are a group") may be formed on the basis of various experiences (e.g., proximity, common fate), in the case of scientists' groups it is almost always based on the perception of similarity. The perception of similarity is usually derived from common beliefs in similar, or even same ideas. These beliefs, which serve as a basis for group formation, are formulated by one or several scientists. Once the beliefs are formulated, additional scientists who accept them can join the group. The group can grow, and even become a discipline—the most common group in science.

In this vein, Mullins (1972), elaborating on the development of scientific groups, proposed that they move through four phases on the way to becoming a discipline. In the first phase, called the *paradigm group*, individuals develop a similar viewpoint on a particular problem with or without communication with one another. The second phase, *communication network*, is characterized by increased contact and decreased isolation among scientists who work in the area, still sometimes without interaction. Only in the third phase, *a cluster*, do scientists become self-conscious about their "groupness" and begin to set boundaries around those who are working on their common problem. In this phase they also establish patterns of communication and form norms. The underlying basis for the group emergence in this phase is group beliefs that group members share. They include a view of the group's own history and a set of theories labelled as "dogma." In the last phase, *specialty*, the group goes through institutionalized by developing a regulated process of training, recruitment of new members, and formalized ways of communication through journals and meetings.

One example of how a new group is formed on the basis of group beliefs is the development of the phage group, which established molecular biology (see Mullins, 1972). In this case, the group beliefs pertained to the functions, structure, and processes of DNA and RNA (Stent, 1968). Specifically, they stated

> . . . that DNA achieves both autocatalytic and heterocatalytic functions by serving as a template for the synthesis of replica polynucleotide chains, through the formation of complementary hydrogen bonds – DNA chains for the autocatalytic, and RNA chains for the heterocatalytic functions. To complete the heterocatalytic functions, the replica RNA chains are translated into polypeptides by the way of a genetic code, under which any given short permulation of three nucleotides along the RNA chain represents one of the standard 20 amino acids. (Stent, 1968, p. 394)

On the basis of these group beliefs, the group functioned. Group members performed studies, exchanged papers, collaborated in their research, organized meetings, and even developed specific patterns of common research and life-style (e.g., concentration on few but excellent papers, camping in nature).

In this case, as in other cases, group beliefs functioned as a symbol for defining group identity and as a glue for the group solidarity (Mullins, 1972). In fact, as it happened in the phage group, a basis for the formation of a scientific group has to be a realization by several scientists that they share the same idea(s). Only subsequently may they set parameters for the group organization.

Changes of Scientists' Group Beliefs

Group beliefs of scientists are subject to the same processes as group beliefs of other groups. They may change, serve as a basis to formation of subgrouping, split, or even disintegrate. All these processes, taking place in scientific groups, can be discussed within the framework of the present conception.

Changes of group beliefs are of special interest, since they often have implications for the development of science. Such implications are especially obvious when group beliefs (and their change) pertain to theoretical or conceptual content. Then, a change of group beliefs indicates a modification of a theory, a conception, or some other premise. A change of group beliefs, either through peaceful modification or through emergence of a new group with new group beliefs, indicates that new scientific beliefs are formulated. It shows that a group of scientists agrees to share different beliefs than those previously held.

A change of group beliefs is not surprising in view of the relative openness of science. That is, science by its nature is characterized by criticism, skepticism, disinterestedness, tolerance, and attempts to innovate (Lakatos & Musgrave, 1970; Merton, 1973). These characteristics imply that group beliefs usually do not freeze. A freezing of group beliefs implies stagnation and fixation, which negate the nature of science. The nature of science requires a constant unfreezing of group beliefs. Although it is hard to judge whether every change in group beliefs indicates progress, it is definitely possible to say that a change indicates extension of knowledge, because it usually implies an emergence of new ideas. In this vein, it is interesting to note that Crane (1969) found that scientists are more committed to advancing ideas than to their group. The groups serve as means for communication, while innovation is the name of the game in scientific groups.

The above characterization of science should not imply that scientists always are open for changes. Even in the present century, groups of scientists have persistently and obstinately adhered to their group beliefs without considering alternatives. Barber (1961) provided several notable examples of resistance by scientists to new ideas in physical and natural sciences. Among them are objections to Lister's theory of antisepsis, Mendel's theory of genetic inheritance, and Arrhenius' theory of electrolytic dissociation.

Groups of scientists may develop a closed system in order to maintain group beliefs among group members. Krantz (1972), for example, referred to "scientific schools" as groups whose members uncritically accept group beliefs, usually that of the leader. He described the case of the operant conditioning school, which has been based on the group beliefs developed by B.F. Skinner. The group formed a relatively isolated system with its own set of ideas, own set of criteria for acceptable research and scientific significance, and little openness to alternatives.

In some groups, changes of group beliefs are accompanied by internal struggle. As in other types of groups, members of scientists groups may bitterly fight for a change, form subgroups, and even split from a parent group. A split indicates that at least two subgroups of scientists did not agree about changing group beliefs, which could refer to certain theory, methodology, or an essence of a discipline. When such disagreement is irreconcilable, the subgroup may part and establish a new group. Among the most known splits in scientific groups are the departures and expulsions in the Freudian group of psychoanalysis. The case of Jung is probably one of the most salient (Murphy & Kovach, 1972).

Carl Jung, a psychiatrist from Zurich, moved close to the psychoanalytic group lead by Freud and within short time was considered as one of its members. Moreover, Freud considered Jung as a possible heir to his leadership (Roazen, 1971). It is beyond the scope of this analysis to describe in details the dispute between Freud and Jung, nevertheless, it focused on basic disagreements, such as Jung's rejection of Freud's emphasis on the role of sexuality in human development. In this disagreement, Jung reinterpreted the significance of Freud's Oedipus complex and reconceptualized the meaning of libido. Jung also wanted to get away from Freud's concentration on causes from the past, and had a different conception of the unconscious.

The final break between Freud and Jung took place in the Psychoanalytic Congress held in Munich in September, 1913. Seven years after the first exchange of letters between them, it became clear that Jung did not accept some of the basic group beliefs of Freud's group and therefore could not continue to be a group member. Jung's presentation at the Congress, "A Contribution to Psychological Types," depicted an alternative view of individuals' psychology to Freud's orientation. Although Jung was reelected as a president of the International Psychoanalytic Association, Freud made it clear that Jung could not continue to be a group member. In Freud's essay in the association's journal, *Jahrbuch*, on the history of the psychoanalytic movement, Jung was described as an outcast of the group. Freud explained why Jung was regarded as seceding from psychoanalysis. Thereafter, the split became a reality. Jung resigned his presidency in April 1914, and 3 months later withdrew from the International Psychoanalytic Association, along with almost the entire body of Swiss analysts, forming his own group.

Conclusions

The presented analysis of scientists' group beliefs indicates that their study is an important direction of emphasis in the sociology and philosophy of science. This focus may contribute not only to the understanding of how groups of scientists organize themselves and change, but also to how scientific ideas develop. Scientific ideas often serve as group beliefs and therefore their examination may shed light on why some ideas persist and others disappear. As a support to what has been just said, I would like to end this postscript with Kuhn's (1970) last sentences from his now classic book, *The structure of scientific revolutions*:

> How does one elect and how is one elected to membership in a particular community, scientific or not? What is the process and what are the stages of socialization to the group? What does the group collectively see as its goals; what deviations, individual or collective, will it tolerate; and how does it control the impermissible observation? A fuller understanding of science will depend on answers to other sorts of questions as well, but there is no area in which more work is so badly needed. Scientific knowledge, like language, is intrinsically the common property of a group or else nothing at all. To understand it we shall need to know the special characteristics of the groups that create and use it. (pp. 209–210)

References

Abelson, R.P., Aronson, E., McGuire, W.J., Newcomb, T.M., Rosenberg, M.J., & Tannenbaum, P.H. (Eds.). (1968). *Theories of cognitive consistency: A source book*. Chicago:
Rand McNally.

Aberle, D.F., Cohen, A.K., Davis, A.K., Levy, M.J., & Sutton, F.X. (1950). The functional
prerequisite of a society. *Ethics, 60*, 100-111.

Adorno, T.W., Frenkel-Brunswick, E., Levinson, D.J., & Sanfood, R.N. (1950). *The
authoritarian personality*. New York: Harper & Row.

Allen, V.L., & Wilder, D.A. (1975). Categorization, belief similarity, and intergroup discrimination. *Journal of Personality and Social Psychology, 32*, 971-977.

Allen, V.L., & Wilder, D.A. (1979). Group categorization and attribution of belief similarity.
Small Group Behavior, 10, 73-80.

Allen, W.S. (1965) *The Nazi seizure of power: The experience of a single German town,
1930-1935*. Chicago: Quadrangle Book.

Allport, F.H. (1924a). *Social psychology*. Boston: Houghton Mifflin.

Allport, F.H. (1924b). The group fallacy in relation to social science. *Journal of Abnormal
and Social Psychology, 19*, 60-73.

Allport, G.W. (1954). The historical background of modern social psychology. In G. Lindzey
(Ed.), *The handbook of social psychology* (Vol. 1, pp. 3-56). Cambridge, MA: Addison-
Wesley.

Allport, G.W. (1968). The historical background of modern social psychology. In G. Lindzey
& E. Aronson (Eds.). *The handbook of social psychology* (2nd ed., Vol. 1, pp. 1-80). Reading, MA: Addison-Wesley.

Allport, G.W. (1985). The historical background of social psychology. In G. Lindzey & E.
Aronson (Eds.), *The handbook of social psychology* (3rd ed., Vol. 1, pp. 1-46). New York:
Random House.

Almond, G., & Verba, S. (1965). *The civic culture*. Boston: Little Brown.

Apter, D.E. (1964). Ideology and discontent. In D.E. Apter (Ed.), *Ideology and discontent*
(pp. 15-46). London: Collier McMillan.

Ardener, S. (1983). Arson, nudity and bombs among the Canadian Doukhobors: A question
of identity. In G.M. Breakwell (Ed.), *Threatened identities* (pp. 239-266). Chichester:
John Wiley & Sons.

Asch, E.S. (1952). *Social psychology*. Englewood Cliffs, NJ: Prentice Hall.

Axelrod, R. (1976). The analysis of cognitive maps. In R. Axelrod (Ed.), *Structure of decision*
(pp. 55-73). Princeton: Princeton University Press.

Barber, B. (1961). Resistance by scientists to scientific discovery. *Science, 134*, 596-602.

Bar-Tal, D. (1984). American study of helping behavior: What, why, and where. In E. Staub, D. Bar-Tal, J. Karylowski, & J. Reykowski (Eds.), *Development and maintenance of prosocial behavior* (pp. 5–27). New York: Plenum.

Bar-Tal, D. (1986). The Masada Syndrome: A case of central belief. In N. Milgram (Ed.), *Stress and coping in time of war* (pp. 32–51). New York: Brunner/Mazel.

Bar-Tal, D. (1988). Delegitimizing relations between Israeli Jews and Palestinians: A social psychological analysis. In J. Hoffman (Ed.), *Arab-Jewish relations in Israel* (pp. 217–248). Bristol, IN: Wyndham Hall Press.

Bar-Tal, D. (1989a). *The contents and origins of the Israeli security beliefs.* Manuscript submitted for publication.

Bar-Tal, D. (1989b). *American convictions about conflictive USA-USSR relations: A case of group beliefs.* Manuscript submitted for publication.

Bar-Tal, D. (1989c). Delegitimization: The extreme case of stereotyping and prejudice. In D. Bar-Tal, C. Graumann, A.W. Kruglanski, & W. Stroebe (Eds.), *Stereotyping and prejudice: Changing conceptions* (pp. 169–182). New York: Springer-Verlag.

Bar-Tal, D. (in press-a). Israel-Palestinian conflict: A cognitive analysis. *International Journal of Intercultural Relations.*

Bar-Tal, D. (in press-b). Causes and consequences of delegitimization: Models of conflict and ethnocentrism. *Journal of Social Issues.*

Bar-Tal, D., & Antebi, D. (1989). *Israeli siege mentality.* Manuscript submitted for publication.

Bar-Tal, D., Bar-Tal, Y., Geva, N., & Yarkin-Levin, K. (in press). Planning and performing interpersonal interaction: A cognitive-motivational approach. In W. Jones & D. Perlman (Eds.), *Advances in personal relationships* (Vol. 2). Greenwich, CT: JAI Press.

Bar-Tal, D., & Geva, N. (1985). A cognitive basis of international conflicts. In S. Worchel & W.B. Austin (Eds.), *The social psychology of intergroup relations.* (2nd ed., pp. 118–133). Chicago: Nelson-Hall.

Bar-Tal, D., & Kruglanski, A.W. (Eds.) (1988). *The social psychology of knowledge.* Cambridge: Cambridge University Press.

Bar-Tal, D., Kruglanski, A.W., & Klar, Y. (1989). Conflict termination: An epistemological analysis of international cases. *Political psychology, 10,* 233–255.

Bar-Tal, D., & Saxe, L. (in press). Acquisition of political knowledge: A social psychological view. In O. Ichilov (Ed.), *Political socialization for democracy.* New York: Teachers College Press.

Bar-Tal, Y. (1989a). Can leaders change followers stereotypes? In D. Bar-Tal, C. Grauman, A.W. Kruglanski, & W. Stroebe (Eds.), *Sterotyping and prejudice: Changing conceptions* (pp. 225–242). New York: Springer-Verlag.

Bar-Tal, Y. (1989b). What can we learn from Fiedler's contingency model? *Journal for the Theory of Social Behavior, 19,* 79–96.

Bar-Tal, Y., & Bar-Tal, D. (in press). Decision making models of helping behavior: Process and contents. In W.M. Kurtines & J.L. Gewirtz (Eds.), *Handbook of moral behavior and development* (Vol. 2). Hillsdale, NY: Lawrence Erlbaum.

Barritt, D.P., & Carter, C.R. (1972). *The Northern Ireland problem* (2nd ed.). Oxford: Oxford University Press.

Barth, F. (1969a). Introduction. In F. Barth (Ed.), *Ethnic groups and boundaries* (pp. 9–38). Boston: Little, Brown and Company.

Barth, F. (1969b). Pathan identify and its maintenance. In F. Barth (Ed.), *Ethnic groups and boundaries* (pp. 117–134). Boston: Little, Brown and Company.

Bartlett, F.C. (1932). *Remembering.* Cambridge: Cambridge University Press.

Bauer, Y. (1982). *A history of the Holocaust.* New York: F. Watts.

Bekterev, V.N. (1921). *Collective reflexology.* (E. Lockwood, Trans., L. Strickland, Ed.). Petrograd: Kolos Publishing House.

Bell, D. (1952) The background and development of Marxian socialism in the United States. In D.D. Egbert & S. Persons (Eds.), *Socialism and American life* (Vol. 1, pp. 213–405). Princeton: Princeton University Press.

Bem, D.J. (1970). *Beliefs, attitudes, and human affairs*. Belmont, CA: Brooks/Cole.

Berger, P.L., & Luckmann, T. (1966). *The social construction of reality*. New York: Anchor Books.

Bernstein, G. (1973). *Anti-Semitism in imperial Germany "1871–1914": Selected documents*. Unpublished doctoral dissertation, Columbia University, New York.

Billig, M. (1978). *Fascists: A social psychological view of the National Front*. London: Academic Press.

Billig, M., & Tajfel, H. (1973). Social categorization and similarity in intergroup behaviour. *European Journal of Social Psychology, 3*, 27–52.

Blumberg, H.H., Hare, A.P., Kent, V., & Davies, M.F. (Eds.) (1983). *Small groups and social interaction* (Vols. 1 and 2). Chichester: John Wiley & Sons.

Blume, S.S. (1974). *Toward a political sociology of science*. New York: The Free Press.

Borhek, J.T., & Curtis, R.F. (1975). *A sociology of beliefs*. New York: John Wiley & Sons.

Bovard, E. (1951). Group structure and perception. *Journal of Abnormal and Social Psychology, 46*, 389–405.

Bracher, K.D. (1971). *The German dictatorship*. London: Weidenfeld and Nicholson.

Bramsted, E.K. (1965). *Goebbels and National Socialist propaganda 1925–1945*. East Lansing: Michigan State University Press.

Bransford, J.D. (1980). *Human cognition*. Belmont, CA: Wadsworth.

Brewer, M.B. (1979). In-group bias in the minimal intergroup situation: A cognitive-motivational analysis. *Psychological Bulletin, 86*, 307–324.

Bruner, J.S., Goodnow, J.J., & Austin, G.A. (1956). *A study of thinking*. New York: Wiley.

Brunswick, E. (1956) *Perception and the representative design of psychological experiments*. Berkeley: University of California Press.

Campbell, D.T. (1958). Common fate, similarity, and other indices of the status of aggregates of persons as social entities. *Behavioral Science, 3*, 14–25.

Cannon, T. (1973). Black Panther party program: What we want, what we believe. In R.R. Evans (Ed.), *Social movements* (pp. 395–401). Chicago: Rand McNally.

Cartwright, D. (1968). The nature of group cohesiveness. In D. Cartwright & A. Zander (Eds.), *Group dynamics: Research and theory* (3rd ed., pp. 21–109). New York: Harper & Row.

Cartwright, D., & Zander, A. (Eds.). (1968). *Group dynamics: Research and theory*. (3rd ed.). New York: Harper & Row.

Charters, W.W., Jr., & Newcomb, T.M. (1952). Some attitudinal effects of experimentally increased salience of a membership group. In G.E. Swanson, T.M. Newcomb, & E.L. Hartley (Eds.), *Reading in social psychology* (rev. ed., pp. 415–420). New York: Holt.

Cohn, N. (1967). *Warrant for genocide*. London: Eyre and Spottiswoode.

Coleman, L. (1941). What is American? A study of alleged American traits. *Social Forces, 19*, 492–499.

Converse, P.E. (1964). The nature of belief systems on mass publics. In D.E. Apter (Ed.), *Ideology and discontent* (pp. 206–261). New York: Free Press.

Coser, L. (1954). Sects and sectarians. *Dissent, 1*, 360–369.

Crane, D. (1969). Social structure in a group of scientists: A test of the "invisible college" hypothesis. *American Sociological Review, 34*, 335–352.

Crane, D. (1972). *Invisible colleges: Diffusion of knowledge in scientific communities*. Chicago: University of Chicago Press.

D'Andrade, B.G. (1984). Cultural meaning systems. In R.A. Shweder & R.A. LeVine (Eds.), *Culture theory* (pp. 88–119). Cambridge: Cambridge University Press.

Dawidowicz, L.S. (1975). *The war against the Jews 1933–1945*. New York: Holt, Rinehart and Winston.

Dawson, P.A. (1979). The formation and structure of political belief systems. *Political Behavior, 1*, 99–122.

Deconchy, J.P. (1984). Rationality and social control in orthodox systems. In H. Tajfel (Ed.), *The social dimension: European developments in social psychology* (Vol. 1, pp. 425–445). Cambridge: Cambridge University Press.

Deutsch, M. (1968). The effects of cooperation and competition upon group process. In D. Cartwright & A.Z. Lander (Eds.), *Group dynamics: Research and theory* (3rd ed., pp. 461–482). New York: Harper & Row.

DeVos, G. (1975). Ethnic pluralism: Conflict and accommodation. In G. DeVos & L. Romanucci-Ross (Eds.), *Ethnic identity.* Palo Alto, CA: Mayfield.

Diamond, M. (1976). The American idea of man: The view from the founding. In T. Kristol & P Weaver (Eds.), *The Americans: 1976* (Vol. 2, pp. 1–24). Lexington, MA: Lexington Books.

DiRenzo, G.J. (Ed.) (1974). *Personality and politics.* Garden City, NY: Anchor Books.

Dollard, J., et al. (1939). *Frustration and aggression.* New Haven: Yale University Press.

Dougherty, J.W.D. (Ed.). (1985). *Directions in cognitive anthropology.* Urbana: University of Illinois Press.

Downey, G.L. (1986). Ideology and the Clamshell identity: Organizational dilemmas in the anti-nuclear power movement. *Social Problems, 33,* 357–373.

Durkheim, E. (1898). Representations individuelles et representations collectives. *Revue de metaphysique, 6,* 274–302. (D.F. Pocock, Trans. *Sociology and philosophy.* New York: Free Press, 1953).

Durkheim, E. (1933). *The division of labor in society* (G. Simpson, Trans.). New York: Mac-Millan.

Durkheim, E. (1951). *Suicide* (J.A. Spaulding & G. Simpson, Trans.). Glencoe, IL: Free Press.

Durkheim, E. (1953). *Sociology and philosophy* (D. Pocock, Trans.). New York: The Free Press.

Duvenger, M. (1954). *Political parties, their organization and activity in the modern state.* New York: Wiley.

Eldersveld, S.J. (1964). *Political parties: A behavioral analysis.* Chicago: Rand McNally.

Emerson, R. (1960). *From empire to nation.* Cambridge: Harvard University Press.

Epstein, A.L. (1978). *Ethos and identity.* London: Tavistock Publications.

Etzioni, A. (1975a). *A comparative analysis of complex organizations.* New York: The Free Press.

Etzioni, A. (1975b). *Complex organizations* (rev. ed.). New York: The Free Press.

Farr, R.M., & Moscovici, S. (Eds.). (1984). *Social representations.* Cambridge: Cambridge University Press.

Festinger, L. (1950). Informal social communication. *Psychological Review, 57,* 271–282.

Festinger, L., Riecken, H.W., & Schachter, S. (1956). *When prophecy fails.* New York: Harper & Row.

Festinger, L., Schachter, S., & Back, K.W. (1950). *Social pressures in informal groups.* New York: Harper.

Festinger, L., & Thibaut, J. (1951). Interpersonal communication in small groups. *Journal of Abnormal and Social Psychology, 46,* 92–99.

Feyerabend, P.K. (1981). *Problems of empiricism* (Vol. 2). Cambridge: Cambridge University Press.

Fishbein, M. (1963). An investigation of the relationship between beliefs about an object and the attitude toward that object. *Human Relations, 16,* 233–240.

Fishbein, M., & Ajzen, I. (1975) *Belief, attitude, intention and behavior.* Reading, MA: Addison-Wesley.

Fisher, C.S. (1967). The last invariant theorists: A sociological study of the collective biographies of mathematical specialists. *European Journal of Sociologists, 8,* 216–244.

Fiske, S.T., & Taylor, S.E. (1984). *Social cognition.* New York: Random House.

Fletcher, G.J.O. (1984). Psychology and common sense. *American Psychologist, 30,* 203–213.

Forgas, J.P. (1981). Epilogue: Everyday understanding and social cognition. In J.P. Forgas (Ed.), *Social cognition* (pp. 259–272). London: Academic Press.

Freud, S. (1960). *Group psychology and the analysis of the ego.* New York: Bantam Books.

Freud, S. (1961). *The standard edition of the complete psychological work of Sigmund Freud.* London: The Hogarth Press.

Galanter, M. (1980). Psychological induction into the large-group: Findings from a modern religious sect. *American Journal of Psychiatry, 137,* 1574-1579.

Geertz, C. (1973). *The interpretation of cultures.* New York: Basic Books.

Gehlen, M.P. (1969). *The Communist Party of the Soviet Union: A functional analysis.* Bloomington: Indiana University Press.

George, A.L. (1969). The "operational code" approach to the study of political leaders: John Foster Dulles' philosophical and instrumental beliefs. *International Studies Quarterly, 13,* 190-222.

Gergen, K.J. (1973). Social psychology as history. *Journal of Personality and Social Psychology, 26,* 309-320.

Gergen, K.J. (1982). *Toward transformation in social knowledge.* New York: Springer-Verlag.

Gillin, J. (1955). National and regional cultural values in the United States. *Social forces, 34,* 107-113.

Glaser, H. (1964). *The cultural roots of National Socialism.* Austin: University of Texas Press.

Golembiewski, R.T. (1962). *The small group.* Chicago: The University of Chicago Press.

Gordon, S. (1984). *Hitler, Germans and the "Jewish Question."* Princeton: Princeton University Press.

Graumann, C.F., & Moscovici, S. (Eds.). (1986). *Changing conceptions of crowd mind and behavior.* New York: Springer-Verlag.

Green, T.H. (1900). Lectures on the principles of political obligation. In *Collected Works* (Vol. 2). London: Longmans, Green.

Griffin, R.W., Skivington, K.E., & Moorhead, G. (1987). Symbolic and interactional perspective on leadership: An integrative framework. *Human Relations, 40,* 199-218.

Griffiths, A.P. (Ed.). (1967). *Knowledge and beliefs.* London: Oxford University Press.

Gusfield, J.R. (1955). Social structure and moral reform: A study of the Woman's Christian Temperance Union. *American Journal of Sociology, 61,* 221-232.

Halmos, P. (1957). Nicolas Bourbaki. *Scientific American, 196,* 88-99.

Hamilton, R.F. (1982) *Who voted for Hitler?* Princeton: Princeton University Press.

Hare, A.P. (1976). *Handbook of small group research* (2nd ed.). New York: The Free Press.

Hartmann, D.D. (1984). Anti-Semitism and the appeal of Nazism. *Political Psychology, 5,* 635-642.

Heider, F. (1958). *The psychology of interpersonal relations.* New York: Wiley.

Higgins, E.T., & King, G. (1981). Accessibility of social constructs: Information-processing consequences of individual and contextual variability. In N. Cantor & J.F. Kihlstrom (Eds.), *Personality, cognition, and social interaction* (pp. 69-121). Hillsdale, NJ: Lawrence Erlbaum.

Hintikka, J. (1962). *Knowledge and beliefs.* Ithaca: Cornell University Press.

Hogg, M.A., & Turner, J.C. (1985). Interpersonal attraction, social identification, and psychological group formation. *European Journal of Social Psychology, 15,* 51-66.

Holsti, O.R. (1962). The belief system and national images: A case study. *Journal of Conflict Resolution, 6,* 244-252.

Homans, G. (1950). *The human group.* New York: Harcourt Brace.

Horwitz, M., & Rabbie, J.M. (1989). Stereotypes of groups, group members, and individuals in categories: A differential analysis. In D. Bar-Tal, C.F. Graumann, A.W. Kruglanski & W. Stroebe (Eds.), *Stereotyping and prejudice: Changing conceptions* (pp. 105-129). New York: Springer-Verlag.

Hostetler, J.A. (1968). *Amish society* (rev. ed.). Baltimore: John Hopkins Press.

Indik, B.P. (1965). Organization size and member participation: Some empirical tests of alternative explanations. *Human Relations, 18,* 339-350.

Israel, J., & Tajfel, H. (1972). *Context of social psychology: A critical assessment.* London: Wiley.

Jackel, E. (1981). *Hitler's world view.* Cambridge: Cambridge University Press.

Jackson, J. (1965). Structural characteristics of norms. In I.D. Steiner & M. Fishbein (Eds.), *Current studies in social psychology* (pp. 301-309). New York: Holt, Rinehart and Winston.

James, W. (1902). *The varieties of religious experience: A study in human nature*. New York: Longmans, Green.

Jaros, D., & Grant, L.V. (1974). *Political behavior*. New York: St. Martin's Press.

Jones, E.E., & Gerard, H.B. (1967). *Foundations of social psychology*. New York: Wiley.

Judd, C.H. (1926). *The psychology of social institutions*. New York: MacMillan.

Jung, C.G. (1922). *Collected papers on analytical psychology* (2nd ed.). London: Beilliere, Tindall and Cox.

Jung, C.G. (1959). *The collected works of C.G. Jung: The archetypes and the collective unconscious* (Vol. 9). New York: Pantheon Books.

Jung, C.G. (1983). *The essential Jung*. Princeton: Princeton University Press.

Kagan, J. (1972). Motives and development. *Journal of Personality and social Psychology, 22*, 51-66.

Katz, D. (1960). The functional approach to the study of attitudes. *Public Opinion Quarterly, 24*, 163-204.

Kaufman, G.D. (1960). *Relativism, knowledge, and faith*. Chicago: University of Chicago Press.

Kelley, H.H. (1955). Salience of membership and resistance to change of group-anchored attitudes. *Human Relations, 8*, 275-289.

Kershaw, I. (1985) *The Nazi dictatorship*. London: Edward Arnold.

Killian, L.M. (1964). Social movements. In R.E.L. Faris (Ed.), *Handbook of modern sociology* (pp. 426-455). Chicago: Rand McNally.

Klar, Y., Bar-Tal, D., & Kruglanski, A.W. (1988). Conflict as a cognitive schema. In W. Stroebe, A.W. Kruglanski, D. Bar-Tal, & M. Hewstone (Eds.), *The social psychology of intergroup conflict* (pp. 73-85). New York: Springer-Verlag.

Kluckhohn, C. (1951). Values and value-orientations in the theory of action: An exploration in definition and classification. In T. Parsons & E. Shils (Eds.), *Toward a general theory of action* (pp. 388-433). Cambridge, MA: Harvard University Press.

Korten, D.C. (1962). Situational determinants of leadership structure. *Journal of Conflict Resolution, 6*, 222-235.

Krantz, D.L. (1972). Schools and systems: The mutual isolation of operant and nonoperant psychology as a case study. *Journal of the History of the Behavioral Sciences, 8*, 86-102.

Krech, D., & Crutchfield, R.S. (1948). *Theory and problems of social psychology*. New York: McGraw Hill.

Kruglanski, A.W. (1980). Lay epistemological-process and contents: Another look at attribution theory. *Psychological Review, 87*, 70-87.

Kruglanski, A.W. (1989). *Lay epistemics and human knowledge: Cognitive and motivational bases*. New York: Plenum.

Kuhn, T.S. (1970). *The structure of scientific revolutions* (2nd ed.). Chicago: University of Chicago Press.

Lakatos, I. (1970). Falsification and the methodology of scientific research programs. In I. Lakatos & A. Musgrave (Eds.), *Criticism and the growth of knowledge* (pp. 91-197). Cambridge: Cambridge University Press.

Lakatos, I., & Musgrave, A. (Eds.). (1970). *Criticism and the growth of knowledge*. Cambridge: Cambridge University Press.

Lane, R.E. (1962). *Political ideology*. New York: Free Press.

Lane, R.E. (1973). Patterns of political beliefs. In J.N. Knutson (Ed.), *Handbook of political psychology* (pp. 83-116). San Francisco: Jossey Bass.

Latané, B. (1981). The psychology of social impact. *American Psychologist, 36*, 343-356.

Latané, B., & Wolf, S. (1981). The social impact of majorities and minorities. *Psychological Review, 88*, 438-453.

LeBon, G. (1968). *The crowd: A study of the popular mind* (2nd ed.). Dunwoody, GA: Norman S. Berg. (Originally published in 1895.)

Lehman, E.C., Jr. (1980). Patterns of lay resistance to women in ministry. *Sociological Analysis, 4*, 317–338.

Levine, J.M. (in press). Reaction to opinion deviance in small groups. In P. Paulus (Ed.), *Psychology of group influence: New perspectives*. Hillsdale, NJ: Erlbaum.

Levine, J.M., & Moreland, R.L. (1985). Innovation and socialization in small groups. In S. Moscovici, G. Mugny, & E. Van Avermaet (Eds.), *Perspectives on minority influence* (pp. 143–163). Cambridge: Cambridge University Press.

LeVine, R.A., & Campbell, D.T. (1972). *Ethnocentrism: Theories of conflict, ethnic attitudes and group behavior*. New York: Wiley.

Levy, S.B. (1975). Shifting patterns of ethnic identification among the Hassidim. In J.W. Bennett (Ed.), *The new ethnicity: Perspectives from ethnology* (pp. 25–50). St. Paul, MN: West Publishing.

Lewin, K. (1947). Frontiers in group dynamics. *Human Relations, 1*, 5–41.

Lewin, K. (1948). *Resolving social conflicts*. New York: Harper & Row.

Lewin, K. (1951). *Field theory in social science*. New York: Harper.

Lijphart, A. (1975). *The politics of accommodation: Pluralism and democracy in the Netherlands* (2nd ed.). Berkeley: University of California Press.

Lindley, C. (Ed.). (1985). *Partnership of principle: Writings and speeches on the making of the Alliance by Roy Jenkins*. London: Secker & Warburg.

Maass, A., & Clark, R.D. (1984). Hidden impact of minorities: Fifteen years of minority influence research. *Psychological Bulletin, 95*, 428–450.

Manicas, P.T., & Secord, P.F. (1983). Implications for psychology of the new philsophy of science. *American Psychologist, 38*, 399–413.

Mannheim, K. (1952). *Ideology and utopia*. New York: Harcourt, Brace and Company.

Mannheim, K. (1954). *Ideology and utopia: An introduction to the sociology of knowledge*. New York: Harcourt.

March, J.G., & Simon, H.A. (1958). *Organizations*. New York: John Wiley & Sons.

Markus, H., & Zajonc, R.B. (1985). The cognitive perspective in social psychology. In G. Lindzey & E. Aronson (Eds.), *Handbook of social psychology* (3rd ed., Vol. 1, pp. 137–230). New York: Random House.

Marx, K. (1967). *Capital* (Vol. 1). New York: International Publishers.

McCall, G.G., & Simmons, G.L. (1982). *Social psychology: A sociological approach*. New York: The Free Press.

McCall, M.W., & Lombardo, M.M. (1978). *Leadership: Where else can we go?* Durham: Duke University Press.

McClelland, D.C. (1955). The psychology of mental content reconsidered. *Psychological Review, 62*, 297–320.

McDougall, W. (1920). *The group mind*. New York: G.P. Putnam's Sons.

McDougall, W. (1939). *The group mind* (2nd ed.). Cambridge: Cambridge University Press.

McGinn, C. (1983). *The subjective view*. Oxford: Clarendon Press.

McGrath, J.E., & Altman, I. (1966). *Small group research*. New York: Holt, Rinehart and Winston.

Mead, G.H. (1934). *Mind, self and society*. Chicago: University of Chicago Press.

Merton, R.K. (1957). *Social theory and social structure*. New York: Free Press.

Merton, R.K. (1973). *The sociology of science*. Chicago: University of Chicago Press.

Merton, R.K. (1973). The normative structure of science. In N.W. Stored (Ed.), *The sociology of science: Theoretical and empirical investigations* (pp. 267–278). Chicago: University of Chicago Press.

Messinger, S.L. (1955). Organizational transformation: A case study of a declining social movement. *American Sociological Review, 20*, 3–10.

Miller, G.A., Galanter, E., Pribram, K.H. (1960). *Plans and the structure of behavior*. New York: Holt.

Milton, S. (1980). Artists in the third Reich. In H. Friedlander & S. Milton (Ed.), *The Holocaust: Ideology, bureaucracy, and genocide*. Millwood, NY: Kraus International Publications.

Moreland, R.L. (1987). The formation of small groups. In C. Hendrick (Ed.), *Review of Personality and Social Psychology* (Vol. 8, pp. 80–110). Beverly Hills, CA: Sage.

Moreland, R.L., & Levine, J.M. (1982). Socialization in small groups: Temporal changes in individual-group relations. In L. Berkowitz (Ed.), *Advances in experimental social psychology* (Vol. 15, pp. 137–192). New York: Academic Press.

Moscovici, S. (1961). *La psychanalyse, son image et son public*. Paris: Presses Universitaires de France.

Moscovici, S. (1976). *Social influence and social change*. London: Academic Press.

Moscovici, S. (1984). The phenomenon of social representations. In R.M. Farr & S. Moscovici (Eds.), *Social representations* (pp. 3–69). Cambridge: Cambridge University Press.

Moscovici, S., Mugny, G., & Van Avermaet, E. (Eds.). (1985). *Perspectives on minority influence*. Cambridge: Cambridge University Press.

Mosse, G.L. (1964). *The crisis of German ideology*. New York: Grosset and Dunlap.

Mosse, G.L. (1966). *Nazi culture: Intellectual, cultural and social life in the Third Reich*. New York: Grosset & Dunlap.

Mosse, G.L. (1970). *Germans and Jews*. New York: Howard Fertig.

Mosse, G.L. (1978). *Toward the final solution: A history of European racism*. New York: Howard Fertig.

Mugny, G. (1982). *The power of minorities*. London: Academic Press.

Mulkay, M.J. (1977). Sociology of the scientific research community. In I. Spiegel-Rosing & D. de S. Price (Eds.), *Science, technology and society* (pp. 93–148). London: Sage.

Mullins, N.C. (1972). The development of a scientific specialty: The phage group and the origins of molecular biology. *Minerva, 10*, 51–82.

Murphy, G., & Kovach, J.K. (1972). *Historical introduction to modern psychology* (3rd ed.). New York: Harcourt Brace Jovanovich.

Mussolini, B. (1935). *Fascism: Doctrine and institutions*. Rome: Ardita.

Nagata, J. (1981). In defense of ethnic boundaries: The changing myths and charters of Malay identity. In C.F. Keyes (Ed.), *Ethnic change* (pp. 87–116). Seattle: University of Washington Press.

Neisser, U. (1967). *Cognitive psychology*. Englewood Cliffs, NJ: Prentice Hall.

Newcomb, T.M. (1951). Social psychological theory: Integrating individual and social approaches. In J.H. Rohrer & M. Sherif (Eds.), *Social psychology at the crossroads* (pp. 31–49). New York: Harper & Brothers.

Newell, A., & Simon, H.A. (1972). *Human problem solving*. Englewood Cliffs, NJ: Prentice Hall.

Noakes, J., & Pridham, G. (Eds.). (1984). *Nazism 1919–1945: A documentary reader* (Vol. 2 & 3). Exeter, U.K.: University of Exeter.

O'Dea, T.F. (1957). *The Mormons*. Chicago: University of Chicago Press.

Olmsted, M.S. (1959). *The small group*. New York: Random House.

Parsons, T. (1951). *The social system*. Glencoe: Free Press.

Parsons, T. (1968). The position of identity in the general theory of action. In G. Gordon & K.J. Gergen (Eds.), *The self in social interaction* (pp. 11–23). New York: John Wiley & Sons.

Pepitone, A. (1981). Lessons from the history of social psychology. *American Psychologist, 36*, 972–985.

Plato (1899). *Dialogues of Plato*. New York: D. Appleton and Company.

Poole, R. (1972). *Towards deep subjectivity*. New York: Harper & Row.

Popper, K.R. (1959). *The logic of scientific discovery*. New York: Harper & Row.

Popper, K.R. (1963). *Conjectures and refutations*. New York: Harper & Row.

Popper, K.R. (1972). *Objective knowledge: An evolutionary approach*. Oxford: Clarendon.

Power, J. (1981). *Amnesty International*. New York: McGraw Hill.

Price, D.J. de S., & Beaver, D. (1966). Collaboration in an invisible college. *American Psychologist, 2*, 1011–1018.

Pryor, J.B., & Ostrom, T.M. (1987). Social cognition theory of group processes. In B. Mullen & G.R. Goethals (Eds.), *Theories of group behavior* (pp. 147–183). New York: Springer-Verlag.

Pulzer, P.G.J. (1964). *The rise of political anti-Semitism in Germany and Austria*. New York: John Wiley & Sons.

Rabbie, J.M., & Horwitz, M. (1988). Categories versus groups as explanatory concepts in intergroup relations. *European Journal of Social Psychology, 18*, 117–123.

Rayner, S. (1986). The politics of schism: Routinization and social control in the International Socialist/Socialist Workers' Party. *Sociological Review Monographs, 32*, 46–67.

Richards, J. (1973). *Visions of yesterday*. London: Routledge and Kegan Paul.

Rigby, T.H. (1968). *Communist party membership in the U.S.S.R. 1917–1967*. Princeton: Princeton University Press.

Roazen, P. (1971). *Freud and his followers*. New York: New York University Press.

Roberts, D.A. (1971). The Orange Order in Ireland: A religious institution? *British Journal of Sociology, 22*, 269–282.

Rokeach, M. (1960). *The open and closed mind*. New York: Basic Books.

Rokeach, M. (1968). *Beliefs, attitudes and values*. San Francisco: Jossey Bass.

Rokeach, M. (1973). *The nature of human values*. New York: Free Press.

Rokeach, M., & Rothman, G. (1965). The principle of belief congruence and the congruity principle as models of cognitive interaction. *Psychological Review, 72*, 128–143.

Romney, A.K., Weller, S.C., & Batchelder, W.H. (1986). Culture as consensus: A theory of culture and informant accuracy. American *Anthropologist, 88*, 313–338.

Russell, B. (1948). *Human knowledge*. London: George Allen and Unwin.

Ryle, G. (1949). *The concept of mind*. New York: Barnes and Noble.

Salisbury, R.H. (1975). Interest groups. In F.I. Greenstein & N.W. Polsby (Eds.), *Handbook of political science* (Vol. 4, pp. 171–228). Reading, MA: Addison-Wesley.

Sampson, E.E. (1977). Psychology and the American ideal. *Journal of Personality and Social Psychology, 35*, 767–782.

Sarnoff, I. (1960). Psychoanalytic theory and social attitudes. *Public Opinion Quarterly, 24*, 251–279.

Sayers, S. (1985). *Reality and reason*. Oxford: Basil Blackwell.

Schleunes, K.A. (1966). *Nazi policy toward German Jews, 1933–1938*. Unpublished doctoral dissertation, University of Minnesota, Minneapolis.

Scott, W.A., Osgood, D.W., & Peterson, C. (1979). *Cognitive structure: Theory and measurement of individual differences*. New York: Halsted Press.

Seliktar, O. (1986). Identifying a society's belief systems. In M.G. Hermann (Ed.), *Political psychology* (pp. 320–354). San Francisco: Jossey Bass.

Shaw, M.E. (1976). *Group dynamics*. New Delhi: Tata McGraw-Hill.

Shaw, R., & Bransford, J. (1977). *Perceiving, acting, and knowing*. Hillsdale, NJ: Lawrence Erlbaum.

Sherif, M. (1936). *The psychology of social norms*. New York: Harper & Brothers.

Sherif, M. (1951). A preliminary experimental study of inter-group relations. In J.H. Rohrer & M. Sherif (Eds.), *Social psychology at the crossroads* (pp. 388–424). New York: Harper & Brothers.

Sherif, M. (1966). *In a common predicament: social psychology of intergroup conflict and cooperation*. Boston: Houghton Mifflin.

Sherif, M., & Cantril, H. (1947). *The psychology of ego-involvements, social attitudes and identifications*. New York: John Wiley.

Sherif, M., Harvey, O.J., White, B.J., Hood, W.R., & Sherif, C.W. (1961). *Intergroup cooperation and competition: The Robbers Cave experiment*. Norman, OK: University Book Exchange.

Shils, E. (1968). Ideology. In D.L. Sills (Eds.), *International encyclopedia of the social sciences* (Vol. 7, pp. 66–76). New York: The Macmillan Company and the Free Press.

Shipley, P. (Ed.). (1976). *The Guardian directory of pressure groups and representative associations*. London: Wilton House.

Sills, D.L. (1958). *The volunteers*. New York: The Free Press.

Simon, H.A. (1976). Discussion: Cognition and social behavior. In J.S. Carroll & J.W. Payne (Eds.) *Cognition and social behavior* (pp. 253–286). Hillsdale, NJ: Lawrence Erlbaum Associates.

Simpson, G.E. (1955). The Ras Tafari movement in Jamaica: A study of race and class conflict. *Social Forces, 34*, 167–171.

Slater, P.E. (1970). *The pursuit of loneliness*. Harmondsworth, U.K.: Penguin Books.

Smelser, N.J. (1962). *Theory of collective behavior*. New York: The Free Press.

Smelser, N.J. (1967). Introduction. In N.J. Smelser (Ed.) *Sociology: An introduction*. New York: John Wiley & Sons.

Smith, M. (1945). Social situation, social behavior, social group. *Psychological Review, 52*, 224–229.

Smith, M.B. (1968). Personality in politics: A conceptual map with application to the problem of political rationality. In O. Garceau (Ed.), *Political research and political theory* (pp. 77–101). Cambridge, MA: Harvard University Press.

Smith, M.B., Bruner, J.S., White, R.W. (1956). *Opinions and personality*. New York: Wiley.

Solso, R.L. (Ed.). (1973). *Contemporary issues in cognitive psychology*. Washington, D.C.: V.H. Winston & Sons.

Spencer, H. (1900). *The principles of sociology*. (2 volumes). New York: D. Appleton.

Staub, E. (1989). *The roots of evil: The origins of genocide and other group violence*. New York: Cambridge University Press.

Steiner, I.D. (1986). Paradigms and groups. In L. Berkowitz (Ed.), *Advances in experimental social psychology* (Vol. 19, pp. 251–289). New York: Academic Press.

Steinert, M.G. (1977). *Hitler's war and the Germans: Public mood and attitude during the second world war*. Athens, OH: Ohio University Press.

Stent, G.S. (1968). That was molecular biology that was. *Science, 160*, 390–395.

Stogdill, R.M. (1959). *Individual behavior and group achievement*. New York: Oxford University Press.

Stroup, H.H. (1945). *The Jehovah's Witnesses*. New York: Russell & Russell.

Szalay, L.B., & Deese, J. (1978). *Subjective meaning and culture: An assessment through word associations*. Hillsdale, NJ: Lawrence Erlbaum.

Szalay, L.B., & Kelly, R.M. (1982). Political ideology and subjective culture: Conceptualization and empirical assessment. *American Political Science Review, 76*, 585–602.

Tajfel, H. (Ed.). (1978). *Differentiation between groups*. London: Academic Press.

Tajfel, H. (1979). Individuals and groups in social psychology. *British Journal of Social Psychology, 18*, 183–190.

Tajfel, H. (1981). *Human groups and social categories*. Cambridge: Cambridge University Press.

Tajfel, H. (Ed.). (1982). *Social identity and intergroup relations*. Cambridge: Cambridge University Press.

Tajfel, H. (1984). Intergroup relations, social myths and social justice in social psychology. In H. Tajfel (Ed.), *The social dimension: European developments in social psychology* (Vol. 2, pp. 695–715). Cambridge: Cambridge University Press.

Tajfel, H., Flament, C., Billig, M.G., & Bundy, R.P. (1971). Social categorization and intergroup behavior. *European Journal of Social Psychology, 1*, 149–178.

Tajfel, H., & Turner, J.C. (1979). An integrative theory of intergroup conflict. In W.C. Austin & S. Worchel (Eds.), *The social psychology of intergroup relations* (pp. 33–47). Monterey, CA: Brooks/Cole.

Tarde, G. (1907). *Social laws: An outline of sociology*. New York: Macmillan.

Tarde, G. (1969). *On communication and social influence: selected papers*. Chicago: University of Chicago Press.

Thomas, W.I. (1917). The persistence of primary group norms in present-day society and their influence in our educational system. In H.S. Jennings, J.B. Watson, A. Meyer, & W.I. Thomas (Eds.), *Suggestions of modern science concerning education* (pp. 159–197). New York: Macmillan.

Thomas, W.I. (1951). *Social behavior and personality: Contributions of W.I. Thomas to theory and social research.* (Edited by E.H. Volkart.) Westport, CT: Greenwood Press.

Thomas, W.I., & Znaniecki, F. (1958). *The Polish peasant in Europe and America.* New York: Dover.

Thompson, B., & Peterson, J.H. (1975). Mississippi Choctaw identity: Genesis and change. In J.W. Bennett (Ed.), *The new ethnicity: Perspectives from ethnology* (pp. 179–196). St. Paul: West Publishing.

Toch, H. (1965). *The social psychology of social movements.* Indianapolis: Bobbs-Merrill.

Triandis, H.C. (1972). *The analysis of subjective culture.* New York: Wiley-Interscience.

Triandis, H.C. (1976). Social psychology and cultural analysis. In L.H. Strickland, F.R. Aboud, & K.J. Gergen (Eds.), *Social psychology in transition* (pp. 223–241). New York: Plenum.

Triska, J.F. (Ed.). (1962). *Soviet communism: Programs and rules.* San Francisco: Chandler Publishing Company.

Truman, D.B. (1951). *The governmental process.* New York: Alfred A. Knopf.

Turner, J.C. (1987). *Rediscovering the social group.* Oxford: Basil Blackwell.

Turner, J.C., & Giles, H. (1981). *Intergroup behavior.* Oxford: Basil Blackwell.

Turner, J.C., Sachdev, I., & Hogg, M.A. (1983). Social categorization, interpersonal attraction and group formation. *British Journal of Social Psychology, 22,* 227–239.

Turner, R.H., & Killiam, L.M. (1957). *Collective behavior.* Englewood Cliffs, NJ: Prentice Hall.

Vander Zanden, J.W. (1960). The Klan revival. *American Journal of Sociology, 65,* 456–426.

Verba, S. (1961). *Small groups and political behavior.* Princeton: Princeton University Press.

Verba, S. (1965). Conclusion: Comparative political culture. In L.W. Pye & S. Verba (Eds.), *Political culture and political development* (pp. 512–560). Princeton: Princeton University Press.

Warriner, C.K., & Prather, J.E. (1965). Four types of voluntary associations. *Sociological Inquiry, 35,* 138–148.

Weimer, W.B. (1979). *Notes on the methodology of scientific research.* Hillsdale, NJ: Lawrence Erlbaum.

Weiner, B. (1986). *An attributional theory of motivation and emotion.* New York: Springer-Verlag.

Welch, R. (1973). The beliefs and principles of the John Birch Society. In R.R. Evans (Ed.), *Social movements* (pp. 298–302). Chicago: Rand McNally.

White, L.A. (1949). *The science of culture.* New York: Farrar, Straus.

Whitworth, J. (1971). The Bruderhof in England: A chapter in the history of a utopian sect. In M. Hill (Ed.), *A sociological yearbook of religion in Britain, 4* (pp. 84–101). London: SCM Press.

Wiener, N. (1948). *Cybernetics.* New York: Wiley.

Wilder, D.A. (1978). Perceiving persons as a group: Effects on attributions of causality and beliefs. *Social Psychology, 41,* 13–23.

Wilder, D.A. (1986). Social categorization: Implications for creation and reduction of intergroup bias. In L. Berkowitz (Ed.), *Advances in experimental social psychology* (Vol. 19, pp. 291–355). New York: Academic Press.

Wilker, H.R., & Milbrath, L.W. (1970). Political belief systems and political behavior. *Social Science Quarterly, 51,* 477–493.

Williams, R.M., Jr. (1960). *American Society* (2nd ed.). New York: Alfred A. Knopf.

Williams, R.M. (1970). *American Society* (3rd ed.). New York: Alfred A. Knopf.

Wilson, J. (1971). The sociology of schism. In M. Hill (Ed.), *A sociological yearbook of religion in Britain, 4* (pp. 1–20). London: SCM Press.

Wistrich, R. (1985). *Hitler's apocalypse: Jews and the Nazi Legacy.* London: Weidenfeld & Nicolson.

Worchel, S. (1984). *A model of achieving group independence.* Paper presented at the XXIII International Congress of Psychology, Acapulco, Mexico.

Wundt, W. (1916). *Elements of folk psychology.* London: George Allen & Unwin.

Wyer, R.S., & Srull, T.K. (Eds.) (1984). *Handbook of social cognition.* Hillsdale, NJ: Erlbaum.

Wyer, R.S., & Srull, T.K. (1986). Human cognition in its social context. *Psychological Review, 93,* 322–359.

Zald, M.N. (1982). Theological crucibles: Social movements in and of religion. *Review of Religious Research, 23,* 317–336.

Zald, M.N., & Ash, R. (1965). Social movements organizations: Growth, decay and change. *Social Forces, 44,* 327–341.

Zander, A., Stotland, E., & Wolfe, D. (1960). Unity of group, identification with group, and self-esteem of members. *Journal of Personality, 28,* 463–478.

Zeman, Z.A.B. (1964). *Nazi propaganda.* London: Oxford University Press.

Zuckerman, A.S. (1979). *The politics of faction: Christian Democratic rule in Italy.* New Haven: Yale University Press.

Author Index

Subject Index